Barbara & Fred — Grownups Now

Living Fully with
Developmental Disabilities

Lotte Moise

author of

As Up We Grew with Barbara

Cypress House
Fort Bragg, California

Barbara & Fred — Grownups Now:
Living Fully with Developmental Disabilities
Copyright © 1998 Lotte Moise

For information, phone (707) 964-9520.
For bookseller and library sales or VISA and MasterCard orders, please call 800-883-7782. Or write to:
Cypress House
155 Cypress Street
Fort Bragg CA 95437

Publishers' Cataloging-in-Publication Data
Moise, Lotte E.
  Barbara & Fred—grownups now: living fully with developmental disabilities / by Lotte Moise. — 1st ed.
    p. cm.
  Includes bibliographical references and index.
  ISBN 1-882897-08-0 (pbk.)
  1. Mentally handicapped children — United States — Biography.
  2. Mentally handicapped children — Family relationships.
  3. Parents of handicapped children — United States — Biography.
  I. Title. HV894.M643 1997
  649'.152—dc21   97-74323
                                                              CIP

Cover design by Gopa Design & Illustration
Cover illustration by Barbara and Fred

Printed in Canada by Hignell Printing

First Edition

2 4 6 8 9 7 5 3 1

Barbara & Fred — Grownups Now

Barberta 25 you
cotemose
freedwant

First steps, 1956.

Dear Barbara

Two simple words which are truly the reason for continuing this book, for you are a young woman now — dear to our family and friends and valued by those you live and work with. When I wrote about you in 1980 I wished that I could promise you "the good life" as most parents wish it for their offspring. I have continued to wish, and also to work for our common cause of advocacy for those who live with disabilities. I have not been lazy, but occasionally have lulled myself into a sense of security about your future. Again you have been the one to shake me out of my complacency.

Just a short time ago, you helped me take a quantum leap in my own growth and awareness. You put me to shame as you sat next to me in the car and with shaky voice and tears in your eyes poured out your heartache about Fred. Fred, your "sweetie" as you call him, the person with whom you have been living as a loving, solidly loyal and mutually supportive couple for many years, had hurt your feelings by being interested in another woman. You were quite clear in your description of the situation, and answered my questions precisely.

There was this "little girl," as you described her, in one of the other group homes in the neighborhood, who kept calling Fred, and had recently come to your house to visit. "And then they went out together."

"Did you go with them?" I asked.

"No! They went without me." And then the tears really flowed.

I wasn't sure how we — your beloved sister Karen, and the warm and loving counselors where you live — could help you through this rough time, but I know that in your outburst you again taught me a lesson. You shattered my simplistic assumptions that you and Fred would be together as a couple forever, living harmoniously and without glitches. This belief had lulled me into hoping that your relationship with him would give you the sense of belonging and permanence I wished for you when I wrote "As Up We Grew With Barbara" fifteen years ago. What an erroneous and superficial assumption! What an abdication from my belief in you as a woman who experiences the full range of human feelings.

And so you jolted me into updating As Up We Grew with Barbara, making me live up to my New Year's Resolution of 1995.

Many people met you through the earlier book, Barbara, and they often ask about you. "How is Barbara? What is she up to now?" They have heard me talk about you. If they have met you and Fred they may be astonished that our frequently "uptight" and restrictive system actually lets two young people with disabilities live together. But you do. Jointly and with a little bit of help from your friends you have overcome the kind of painful time that can come to any of us. You two continue to be a couple.

So the people who treasure their copy of what you refer to as "my book" (especially when you have co-signed it) will now know what's happened in your life since you were twenty-six.

— Lotte

Contents

Foreword

When almost twenty years ago my wife and I wrote the foreword to Lotte Moise's *As Up We Grew With Barbara,* we said, "This is not just a penetrating, honest, warm and lucid account of this quarter-century of progress seen through the eyes of one family, but it will also serve as a call to action, as a guide on how to face the battles still to be won."

And now we have the unusual opportunity of getting a second look at this family, with Barbara in her forties, very much a person in her own right, sharing her life with Fred, and letting us get a better understanding of how normal it can be to be different.

But this book also tells us a great deal about Lotte Moise, not just as a caring mother, but also as a courageous, high-spirited citizen, a skillful challenger of bureaucracy and indefatigable activist. Her capacity to combine very personal and often intimate thoughts and observations with her own always significant political/sociological commentaries and criticisms give this book a special and enduring quality.

Gunnar Dybwad, Professor Emeritus
Heller Graduate School, Brandeis University

Introduction

Barbara — our third child — developed more slowly than the others. Her presence caused us puzzlement and pain, wondering and warmth, laughter and love — all this with a diagnosis and label of "mental retardation."

Now that she is an adult, we find that she has given us focus, insight, and a more balanced sense of values. As we grew up with Barbara, I found myself writing about her more and more often. I wanted to tell others in the world out there about our discoveries and new perceptions. Parents can and should be the first line of defense for other parents. We can be the dreamers of dreams of ideally appropriate programs for our sons and daughters and at the same time their severest critics.

Since this has turned out to be a very personal book, and in order not to embarrass my family, I asked each of them for permission to describe and quote them. Barbara, too. My question to her was, "Is it all right for me to write a book about you? Including a lot of personal happenings?" She said, "It's okay to write about me. Write it down. The part about me, Chas and Gail (her group home managers) can read too. They do good things for me."

Then I asked her how she thought a book like this could help parents.

"Parents?" she asked. "It might stop them from pushing us around. We want to do things by ourselves!"

So here is Barbara's book. It incorporates the material of the first edition and contains important information of progress and setbacks in the field. It is offered in the hope that other families who have children with developmental special needs may read it, take heart, and wherever and whenever possible, take action.

Chapter 1

Home Is a Moving Out

All three of our children are grown now and live on their own. I'm on my own too since Al, our Dad as I always call him, died in 1981. When the "kids" roll in at odd intervals for short weekends or holiday vacations, their modes of travel reflect their lives. Karen zips in from San Francisco with her sea kayak strapped to the top of her car. She is a successful nurse practitioner. It's a bigger planning effort for David's journey from Seattle. He is married to Judy and has two children, Leah and Jacob. There's never any telling in which of their vehicles they'll arrive, for David seems to have inherited his father's interest in cars. He also followed in Al the printer's footsteps and teaches graphic arts. Barbara travels on our once-a-day bus from Santa Rosa — about a hundred miles south in the adjoining county of Sonoma. The small, colorful van constitutes an invaluable and hard won transportation link from our beautiful coast to the Bay Area of San Francisco, and I am happy to see it coming.

Barbara and her boyfriend Fred usually come together. He helps her as they maneuver their luggage down the steps. Even for a short weekend they tend to pack enough to last for a month. The driver calls a cheerful wish to the two of them, and the three of us bear-hug. For Barbara I have to stretch up; she's taller than I. Also larger around. She wears her dark blond hair in a shaggy cut, becoming to her pert round face with its blue eyes and almost snub nose. Now forty-two, when she tells her age (usually followed by an announcement of her

1

next birthday with the precise day of the week!) people look surprised, as though they think she is younger. She does seem younger, partly because she often speaks in abbreviated sentences. Partly because she zeros in on the core of situations and the essence of people's feelings with the directness of a child.

Like one Christmas years ago when Barbara was home on vacation, excitedly getting ready for houseguests, festivities, and surprises. We were both puttering around the kitchen when there was a knock on the front door. I opened it and there stood Julie, the youngest daughter of old friends who had divorced and reorganized their lives elsewhere. Julie is younger than Barbara and has been one of her staunch supporters since they were little girls. Once, when our children were playing together, we mothers noticed Julie take Barbara by the hand and lead her outside. "Where are you two going?" I asked.

"Out!" said Julie. "I'm going to teach her out of this retarded business."

On that winter day years later, Julie appeared far from confident. Stooped, bedraggled in a dirty peacoat, stringy haired, she looked defeated. I heard she had been messing around with dope, experimenting with men, and trying in a disorganized fashion to find her own way, and I had tried to let her know through her mother that she was welcome to come to our house anytime if she wanted to talk. Now I was glad she had come. Barbara knew nothing of her troubles. She turned around, recognized her old friend and shouted, "Julie Ray!" — and then slowly — "Why are you so sad?" Julie put her head on my shoulder and cried.

It happened again on a visit to the beauty shop. We knew the owner well, and sadly I told Barbara that Roberta's oldest son had been killed in a car crash the preceding week. "I'm not sure if Roberta is back at work yet, Barbara. But if she is, perhaps you had better not talk to her about the accident at all. Her hurt must still be so new and sore."

Barbara nodded in agreement, but as she settled into the chair in front of the mirror, I could see in her reflected face that she would be unable to contain her feelings. She got up and hugged Roberta. "You'll miss him," she said, "but don't cry. Please don't cry anymore!"

Since I am a widow, Barbara's directness now extends itself to my friendships. Not so long ago on a Sunday morning we planned to have brunch with a family friend whom Barbara treasures. Peter is not a married man and after Al died she would occasionally sound him out as a possible replacement dad. Gently he would say, "Barbara, I like your Mom very much. I like you too, but she's a friend, not my girl friend."

For this Sunday morning brunch Barbara and I brought along a house guest of ours and he brought a woman friend. "Now, Barbara," I had tried to coach her. "You know what a private person Peter is. He won't want to talk about his feelings in a public place at breakfast, so don't ask him any personal questions, please." We met outside the restaurant. There were introductions all around, and when Peter introduced his friend to Barbara, out popped her uppermost concern, "Do you really love him?" she asked her.

It has always been like that with Barbara. Her sensitivity and perception far outshine her indistinct speech, the shortcomings of her physical coordination, and her inability to read. She is a neat young woman who takes up her full space in our family configuration.

Why then does she come home for vacations from a distant city?

Barbara did live at home until she was eighteen. Then she too wanted to move out like her sister and brother, who had left for college. Though we now have a Community College branch campus of the College of the Redwoods right here on our headlands, many young people still move out of our small town after they graduate from high school and Al and I had always thought we might lose our children to the big city. There are few job opportunities here on the Mendocino Coast unless you want to work in the lumber mill or the woods, or become a commercial fisherman.

So it seemed the normal state of affairs for our two older children to leave at eighteen. It came as somewhat of a shock, though, when our youngest wanted to do the same thing. We had certainly let her become increasingly self-reliant and independent. She, too, had visited friends' homes overnight. She had gone to summer camp and had even spent a week on campus with her sister and later her brother — each time stashed away rather secretly in the dorm and watched over by helpful classmates.

But because she had special needs, because her pattern of growth had been different from that of her sister and brother, we came close to walking into the trap of parental overprotection, which in our case was the illusion of ownership and permanence. Perhaps we thought she would remain childlike forever and dependent on our everlasting presence. At any rate, she shattered our assumptions with an angry declaration of independence when she was only sixteen.

A neighbor of ours had died of cancer. "Uncle" Fay had been a good friend to our children. Barbara couldn't understand that he was gone: why? how? where? We tried to answer her repeated questions until she no longer asked them. A few weeks later she and I were having an angry round-and-round. I nagged. Barbara balked. Suddenly she looked at me and asked, "When are you going to die, Mummy?"

I was shocked. She was worrying about the one life condition we cannot change for our children with special needs. As I put my arms around her, I assured her I was feeling fine and should be good for a long, long time. "Why do you ask, Barbara?"

"Because then I will be free."

It was the first indication that she viewed us as restraining and oppressive parents. It was her rebellion against being held too close.

The timing was right. I had read about progressive independent living programs in the Scandinavian countries for young adults with mental retardation and wanted to see them with my own eyes. The National Association for Retarded Citizens, an organization of concerned parents and volunteers, supported an annual program of travel grants which enabled three or four U.S. citizens to study mental retardation programs abroad and made it possible for those in other countries to do the same in ours. (Over the years this program has developed into an international fellowship trust, named *The Rosemary F. Dybwad International Fellowship Trust, Inc.* after its founder and has given over 100 awardees a global sharing and learning experience of programs of excellence in our field of endeavor.)

I sent for an application form and wrote a few letters to inquire about specific names and places in Denmark. That is how I met two persons who were to become significant mentors, co-workers and friends.

Professor Rosemary Dybwad, in whose honor the grant program was established, took a personal interest in those of us who applied for a stipend. While her husband, Professor Gunnar Dybwad, served as national executive director during the early years of the national association, she had become aware of an amazing phenomenon. Parent groups working on behalf of children with mental retardation, whom we now include under the term developmental disabilities, were springing up simultaneously in many apparently disconnected parts of the world. To establish links between them, she recruited volunteers who helped her translate newsletters from different languages into English. I volunteered for German and French. Soon there was almost no one in the field that she and Gunnar did not know. At the time I applied for the award Rosemary told me of Robert Perske, a chaplain at the Kansas Neurological Institute, who had just returned from a three-week swing through Denmark, Sweden, and Norway. Perhaps he would share his travel notes with me. Bob turned out to be a generous man to whom the spreading of the word was more important than copyright concerns, and when I had read the diary of his twenty-one day trip and registered the enthusiasm of his voice and long distance phone advice, I knew what I wanted to do. Bob Perske had seen a little bit of everything. I would concentrate on one part of what he had experienced.

Barbara was seventeen when I received the Rosemary Dybwad International Award, and in the fall of 1971 my husband Al, Barbara, her older sister Karen, and I left for Copenhagen. Our twenty-year old son, David, volunteered to stay at home and supervise our printshop.

Just before we left for the trip, our family had reached an important decision. If it was indeed time for Barbara to eventually leave home, perhaps she should have a little house of her own in which to practice this independence. We cleared an area of our property about a stone's throw from the back porch and began to look at plans. We would start to build when we returned.

Denmark made a tremendous impression on us, which I have detailed in a later chapter, but when we returned our cheerful Barbara reverted to a grouchy teenager. At first we thought she was suffering from an acute attack of "circusitis," the dread disease that overcomes people — especially children — who have had too good a time at parties or on vacation. "She'll get over it," we thought. But she did not. Every morning was a struggle to get her off to school on time. After years of yearning to be allowed to ride the yellow school bus, she now complained about riding "with all the little kids." She balked at going to her separate special school. "Why can't I go to junior high?" she wanted to know. Finally she announced in total rebellion, "I hate Fort Bragg! I hate home!"

That did it. We scrapped the idea of building a halfway house in our own backyard and began to plan for her move out of town.

It has not been all smooth sailing either for Barbara or for us. Her first placement in a brand-new family care home in a neighboring county turned into a disaster when the caretaker turned out to be an alcoholic and, to our horror, Barbara was molested. The next placement — with the parents of a schoolmate — was excellent and saw her to the end of the school year. After that she spent four years in a large city residence within close reach of her brother and sister who were working and going to college in the Bay Area. She was contented at first, but when Karen and David moved away, she felt bereft.

It hurt us to hear our daughter say. "I wanna come closer to home," when we had no choices of quality living arrangements in our rural area. After spending a weekend with us, she would drag her heels at bus time until we almost missed it. I felt like gathering her into my arms and saying, "Stay home, girl. Come back and stay with Mom and Dad."

But by that time we knew this was not the answer. At twenty-six she was a young adult with a lifetime ahead of her and young enough to grow and develop and learn.

And grow she did, and still does, and we with her. Time and time again as she returns home we have an opportunity to take a fresh look at her and marvel at the progress she has made. In more ways than one she is a well-rounded person who never looks the same. She is about five foot seven and weighs close to two hundred pounds. With her hour glass shape she takes after Al's mother and sister. Karen and I have always envied her waist and hips, for we tend to be flat in the bustle and over-endowed on top. Barbara is the only blond in a family of brunettes. Her eyes are bright blue and her nose short and straight.

When Barbara is well rested, interested, and happy, you may not notice that she has any problems at all until she speaks. Her language is basic and meaningful, and in spite of short-cut sentences and fuzzy consonants she usually persists until she has made her point. When she is tired, bored or angry she still rounds her shoulders, sticks her thumb in her mouth, and bends over as if she were leaning on it. On happy days her smile is radiant and her expression and touch alive, light and loving.

Over the years, with the help of speech therapy and increasing life experiences, she has improved greatly in her powers of communication. In times of great joy and great stress she surprises me with quantum leaps in the precision and length of her sentences.

It's her unusual walking and running that continue to give her trouble. She has severe orthopedic foot problems and poor general coordination and balance. Her flat feet turn outward, and when she breaks into a run, her arms swing wildly and she bends over at the waist. Too many tumbles have made her more fearful. For years she had to wear heavy braces to support both her ankles and wobbly knees. At the time they were made of steel and leather and attached to husky, high top boots. She put them on faithfully most mornings. We know so much more now about early intervention with physical therapy than was available to her as a small child. I continue to admire her courage and patience as she confronts the hurdles in her life.

We have watched her slowly but surely become more and more responsible, independent, and assertive. She will probably always lag behind her so-called "normal" friends and relations in cognitive skills, but it's hard to beat her in inner warmth, kindness and humanness.

With acceptance of her differences and support for her efforts to learn, we hope that she will continue to strengthen the skills and abilities she needs for survival and with which she can control her environment. Her greater independence from us is the best insurance for her future. We are trying to prepare her for a future without either parent, one for which she will be equipped not only with practical skills, but also with essential emotional strengths.

Like the adult she now is, Barbara lives away from me and her siblings. But as a beloved and welcome daughter, she likes to return to the house on Sherwood Road, and worries about what will happen to it when I die. Another difficult question to answer for her! She loves to go on trips with her peers, and joyfully spends time with her sister and brother wherever they may be.

One time when I was writing and searching for an apt definition of "home," I asked Barbara: "What do you think a good home is, Barbara? How would you describe one?" She thought and replied, "Home is a moving out." Barbara has indeed grown up. We have all grown with her. How it happened is in this book.

"Dad and me going on a plane."

After Europe trip, 1978

Chapter 2

Before Barbara

Al's family roots were in the genteel South of Alabama. As late as the fifties when his mother visited us here in Fort Bragg she always wore a hat and white gloves to go shopping in town, and told us about the slaves who worked for members of her family and how well they were taken care of. I never met Al's father, who died before we met, but Al respected him with one exception: his father had never lost his *lesser than* opinion of Negroes. "I simply had to give up arguing about it with him," Al told me, but the issue clearly strengthened his uncompromising passion for fair treatment of underdogs.

Al was not quite sixteen when he graduated in 1927 into the depth of the depression and left home. He was only twenty when he got married, and soon lost his wife who died in childbirth. The baby, a boy also named Al, was raised by his maternal grandparents, the Bells, who lived in North Dakota. Al Moise rode trains and slept under bridges for a while and then tried to put his life together again. His second marriage ended in divorce shortly before the start of World War II. When Al enlisted, the Bells adopted Young Al whom they had raised so lovingly for nine years. Young Al is now 60, married, and has a daughter who has elevated me to great-grandmotherhood status. We love and stand by each other as family.

I was born at the end of World War I in Duesseldorf, Germany, which is just close enough to the French border to have been influenced directly by the edicts of the Treaty of Versailles. Small as I was, I remember the military occupation. A French officer was billeted in our living room until my little brother was born in 1921. I was not much affected by the postwar political turmoil until the emergence of Nazism in the early thirties. I know now that growing up in "Super Race" Germany in a partly Jewish family gave me a measure of strength without which I might not have been able — much later — to overcome the "borning" of a child who was different.

Kind and concerned friends in England encouraged my parents to send me to a Quaker boarding school where there was a scholarship available. I was reluctant, but when my dad's tennis club denied me junior membership because I didn't have the requisite number of Aryan grandparents, that did it. I knew they played tennis in England. It was a rough adjustment from a warm comfortable home and family. Many a night I soaked homesick tears into my clammy pillow. It wasn't easy to become accepted by my British sixteen-year-old classmates, but the teachers were wonderfully helpful and supportive. My English improved by leaps and bounds and soon I was able to make friends again. I was beginning to appreciate how wonderful it is to learn another language as a window on a culture different from our own.

Later, when Barbara and her friends entered my life, this early learning aided me in understanding their desperate need for tools of communication — be it by speech therapy, sign language, or access to the miracle of computers. Very recently Barbara tried to tell me about something she had seen. I didn't get it and asked her to say it again, and then again. In exasperation she said, "Give me a pen and a paper!" and rapidly drew a little picture — an effective form of communication.

After graduation from school there followed two years at Charlotte Mason College in the Lake District of Northern England. It was physically Spartan to the core and ultra Victorian socially, but an excellent teaching college. The child-centered teaching philosophy of the founder would stand me in good stead when I became involved in the special education needs of children with disabilities.

Our family came to America in 1937. It was the tail end of the Depression and as my father's medical practice grew, I subway-commuted to Columbia University. I graduated with a B.S. in teaching French and German and an M.A. in Student Personnel and Guidance. In March of 1944 I became a proud citizen of the United States. All my life I had worried about war, and hoped there would never be another one. Now my beloved England was being bombed and the scant news of my relatives in Germany was gruesome. I was convinced I had to take part in this war and applied for training at the U.S. Coast Guard Academy — the one branch of the service that served a peacetime purpose I could square with my hopes for world peace. In the SPARS I learned about American women from different parts of the country and from vastly different cultural, educational, religious and moral persuasions. We worked and played together and the respect and affection that grew between us I carried with me into my life as wife, mother and parent advocate for Barbara.

It was in 1946, when I was transferred to Seattle to decommission the SPAR barracks, that I met Al (and his friend Owen, a native of Fort Bragg, who later became the link to our move to the Mendocino Coast). Hard years before and during the war had shaped Al into the man I fell in love with. He had served four years of heavy Navy duty from Patton in North Africa, to the actions at Anzio and Salerno and then the mop-up in the Pacific. He had an incredible sense of confidence and independence, mellowed by charm and a great earthy sense of humor. For me it was love at first sight. This man was so different from the New York academics and professionals I had dated. He expected highest quality from himself and it was never easy for employees, and later for our kids, to measure up to his standards. These high standards were at times difficult hurdles for Karen and David. But for Barbara they translated into positive and hopeful developmental expectations at times when the rest of the world flinched at the words *mental retardation* and set limits of hopelessness for those so labeled.

At the time I met Al he was heading north to Alaska with his friend to seek adventure. I planned to go to summer school in Mexico City and then return to New York. We wrote a lot of letters that year. There was not much long distance phoning between Fairbanks and New

York in the forties and of course no e-mail. When we decided to spend some time together the following year, my father offered no financial aid for his daughter's venture to meet an ex-sailor who lived in a small cabin in Fairbanks and did janitorial work, but I took the train west. Al hitchhiked south. We met! We bought an open war-surplus jeep at a Veterans' Set-Aside Sale and headed north. In 1947 the Alaska Highway had just been opened to civilian traffic, and that four-week camping trip turned out to be a wonderful pre-nuptial honeymoon. We arrived back in Fairbanks happy and ready to get married. I wondered how I might explain this sequence of events to our children-to-be, but they became teenagers in the sixties and took it in stride.

Karen was born in 1949 in St. Joseph's Hospital on the banks of the Chena River in Fairbanks and later that year we packed our belongings into our jeep and headed south. Fort Bragg, California was a diverse community with roots in Finland, Italy, Portugal and the Native American tribes. It was a fishing and logging town — a company town, and we had good neighbors who taught me many country woman skills. I baked and cooked up a storm, and like a squirrel, admired my store of pickles, jams and chutneys on shelves in the storage cabin.

Al had wanted me to be a full-time housewife. His mother thought that life would be much too quiet for us in this small town but changed her mind on subsequent summer visits when our six-party phone line began to ring. In 1950 the Korean War (or "police action") rudely interrupted our peace and quiet. Al, an inactive Navy Reservist, was pulled back into service. He served on Guam while I accepted my folks' invitation to come to New York and let them supervise my second pregnancy and birth. That became David, and when Al came home to claim and meet his son we returned to Fort Bragg.

In 1952 nobody had even heard of Fort Bragg or Mendocino County. I tried to ship some parcels of accumulated treasures ahead to our home address. "You must be mistaken, Ma'am," said the man behind the counter as he shoved the box back towards me. "There's a Fort Bragg in North Carolina — an army base — you must mean that one." I pushed back. "No, I *mean* California. Fort Bragg, California. We live there." I wished I had a photo to show him. He protested again — more gruffly. He was clearly getting irritated at my doubting his postal authority. But I stuck to my guns. "Couldn't you look it up?" Then he disappeared behind a pile of mail sacks and returned with a large directory. He plunked it punishingly on the counter and lo and behold there it was — just about halfway between San Francisco and Eureka on the ocean as I had told him. "You're right!" he admitted. "Never heard of the place before!"

It felt good to come home. Our house had been kept warm and was well taken care of and comfortable. So was our marriage. Al concentrated most of his energies on becoming a fine printer and both of us were increasingly involved in the needs of our home town. His activities ranged from the Chamber of Commerce to the rural volunteer fire district and Nature Conservancy. He was one of a group of concerned citizens who opposed the construction of a nuclear power plant on a fault south of our town. We took part in the exciting development of an art center in neighboring Mendocino. I was drafted by the PTA before Karen and David were even in school. Substitute teaching and an evening class in English for the foreign born who wanted to become citizens kept my teaching credentials alive and once again were step-ups for the future.

And then came Barbara. She was born in December 1953 in the old Redwood Coast Hospital which makes her a Native Daughter of the Golden West. Over the years she has changed our lives and taught me the true meaning of *Community*. It's a concept that I spell with a capital "C" and cling to for her future well being and that of all our sons and daughters with special differences.

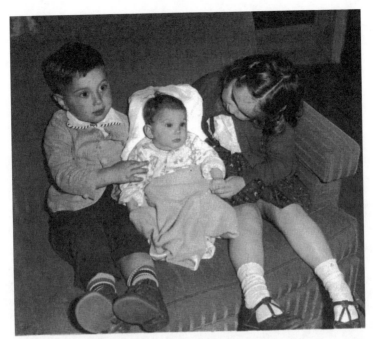

"The baby is me when I was teeny."

Al and Lotte with David, Karen and baby Barbara, 1953

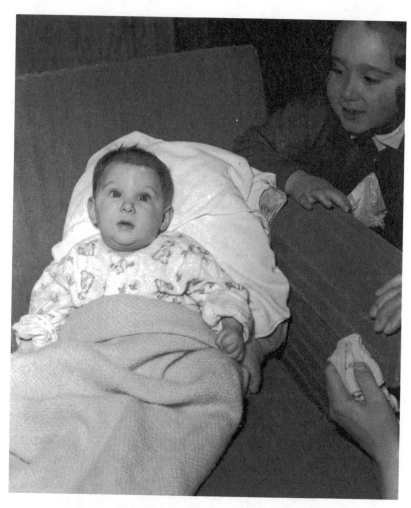

Born December 1953, Barbara with Karen, January 1954

Chapter 3

Third Children Are Easy

I was an old hand at coming home with a baby. "Birthing" care was beginning to change and no longer were women required to stay in the hospital for a week or ten days as had been the case when Karen was born in 1949 in Fairbanks, or David in Manhattan in 1951. Barbara and I were allowed to go home after four days. I felt well rested. My few episiotomy stitches were healing nicely and I was able to get into my gray wool skirt with only a slightly deeper than usual breath.

I was anxious to get home. Al's mother (who was nick-named "Mud" because Al had slurred the "th" in "mother" when he was a little boy) had been impatiently staying with us for more than a week and was taking care of the home front. Christmas was just around the corner, and with two excited preschoolers and a new baby I knew that the next weeks would be hectic. But Barbara nursed well and slept soundly. Karen and David eagerly took turns holding their baby sister and observed and reported her every move. Mud clucked because I would not always retreat into the privacy of our bedroom for the "intimate" feeding process. We felt like a contented, complete family. "Third children are easy," I thought to myself.

During the winter months I was grateful that Baby Barbara lived up to my positive presumptions. She made few demands and that was lucky, for Karen and David suddenly gave us a scare. Fort Bragg's doctors had become aware of a high incidence of tuberculosis among their patients and took steps to look into the situation. A neighbor

17

and former baby-sitter died during TB lung surgery, and all of us (except Barbara who had never been in contact with her) were given skin tests. Karen and David's turned out to be strongly positive and x-rays showed that they had both weathered mild cases of TB. Karen's was completely healed, but David's x-rays still looked doubtful. He was a skinny little two and a half year old just recovering from a strenuous case of measles. While the x-rays were being read locally and by a distant specialist we worried that our little boy *might* have to spend some time in a TB facility out of town. It was a major worry that temporarily diverted me from Barbara. Dr. Lloyd Hall took us through this time calmly and carefully and we were allowed to keep David home. "Give him plenty of TLC and two naps a day." was the order. Spring came, the rain stopped, and all seemed to be well.

Our doctor's family also had two children and an infant and his wife and I became friends — and began simultaneously to suffer from cabin fever. After an early morning phone planning conference we managed marvels of accelerated housework in order to get ready for an outing before noon. Then we'd pack a simple lunch, extra panties and diapers, and pile the babies in banana boxes in the station wagon. These snug cribs are easy to carry by the handholds in each end. We had an endless choice of beaches and state parks where the children could run and play safely. With luck the babies would take naps after lunch and we mothers had a chance for adult conversation. Our banana box outings became happy life savers.

During that spring the first uncomfortable feelings began to invade my consciousness. The Halls' banana box baby was a month and a half older than Barbara, but what a difference. Was it just because he was a boy? At home I reached for Dr. Arnold Gesell's book *(First Five Years of Life)* on child development and looked at the pictures. I did this often, each time more surreptitiously, as if I were afraid of being caught. What I read in the text and saw in the photos didn't make me feel better. Barbara seemed far behind the babies in the book, and although Karen and David had not been junior athletes at her age, I was certain they had been much more active.

Al was of little help to me at this stage. I'm a verbal worrier; I wanted to talk about my observations and concerns. He growled at me every time I touched the subject. "You must be getting old, dear! You never used to worry so when Karen and David were babies. Why don't you relax and enjoy her?" So I put Gesell back on the shelf, way back. Like an addict I hid it behind other books and promised myself not to look at it for at least a month.

Karen was the first member of our family to echo my fears. I was changing Barbara's diaper one day, with Karen kneeling at the south end of the bassinet wielding the powder, when she asked, "Why doesn't our baby ever do anything, Mom?" I was still trying to think of an answer when she continued almost accusingly, "Keith (Hall) rolled off the bed today when Edith changed him." I can't remember what I said, but I know that her question registered as a milestone with me.

My father gave me the next signal on a sunny afternoon later that summer. My parents had arrived to meet their new grandchild. Barbara was eight months old, and my father was an observant physician. We were sitting in the garden when I heard the phone ring. "Here, hold her a minute, please," and I dumped Barbara into my father's lap before dashing for the house. When I returned, Papi was looking at the baby with a bemused look on his face. "You know, Lotte," he said as he gave her back to me, "she should have yelled when you handed her to me so abruptly." My ears heard his words, but my worried heart was not ready to cope with the essence of his message, so I filed away another incident in my cache of gnawing doubts.

By the time Barbara was a year old, I was finding it impossible to ignore those doubts. Why wouldn't she, why couldn't she get going? Madge Relyae, Mendocino County's first public health nurse, came to supper one night and volunteered to check her over. She noted two creases below one buttock but not on the other side, which, she said, might be an indication of a structural congenital hip condition. "This would certainly explain why she isn't crawling or trying to pull herself up to try to walk. Perhaps we should make an appointment for her with California Crippled Children's Services soon."

I took Gesell's book off the shelf one more time and found that the difference between our baby and little Keith Hall had become astronomical. At fourteen months Keith was a buster of a babe. His sturdy legs bowed slightly apart by Pampers, he toddled all over the place — around, over, and under seemingly insurmountable obstacles. He had started to spend occasional overnights with us, and in the morning he'd lift himself onto a small chair in the kitchen, where he sat howling impatiently and pounding the table with his spoon until I managed to put a bowl of hot cereal in front of him.

Barbara, on the other hand, was patience personified. She rarely cried for her food, though she tackled it vigorously once it was served and had learned to feed herself. She was able to roll from her tummy to her back but couldn't turn the other way, and she sat up only when we propped her up against a solid object. She showed her pleasure of recognition with a big smile and body wiggle — the most enthusiastic one for her daddy. We had to childproof the house for Keith because everything went into his mouth, while Barbara sat surrounded by her toys and was just now trying to grasp objects with her hands. I put away the old playpen as an unnecessary restraint. I knew in my heart of hearts that I would cheer her on the day that she started to "get into things."

The chickenpox siege during the next spring brought matters to a head. All three of our children caught it — Karen first, David next, and then Barbara. Each of them waited their turn for the full twenty-one day incubation period and I felt as if I had been "Nurse Nancy" forever. One morning our family doctor dropped by for a housecall. He dispensed pills and expert advice and then settled down for a cup of coffee. "Aside from the chickenpox, Lloyd," I ventured wearily, "what do you think of Barbara's overall development now?" "Why don't you leave Lloyd alone," roared my husband. "Can't you let him have his coffee in peace?"

"Now wait a minute, Al," said Lloyd. "Barbara is fifteen months old, and I think many a mother would have rushed her child down to the University of California Hospital long before this."

We talked. We made plans. We took steps. Of course I was still afraid, but my fears were being validated and that made them not quite as threatening as before. I felt a little better because we were finally doing something for Barbara.

The first stop on the odyssey was an appointment with Dr. Peck, a pediatrician in Santa Rosa, one hundred and ten miles from home. Barbara was seventeen months old now. She was still not walking and quite heavy. I gratefully accepted my neighbor Olga's offer to come along and help me. It was a long, tiring trip. Dr. Peck asked endless questions and seemed to be going over Barbara with a fine-toothed comb. Then he referred her for x-rays of her hips, and of her head which appeared to him to be abnormally small, and to a neurologist for further tests. We had to spend a night in a motel and I learned to make a bed on the floor of the closet as a safe alternative to a crib. The next morning we returned to Dr. Peck's office.

"There is much that is normal about your little girl," he began reassuringly. "Her hips and lower spine seem to be okay, but there are a few things to be concerned about." He showed me the skull x-rays which had been essentially nonconclusive for whatever he was looking for. During the night I had remembered something about Young Al, my husband's first-born son by a previous marriage. While I knew that my own head and my husband Al's were on the large side, Young Al had once jokingly referred to his own "pointed head" for which the Navy had found it difficult to find a small enough hat. Dr. Peck was interested in this bit of hereditary information, and eventually the worry about a possible diagnosis of microcephaly faded. "I would like to refer you to a specialist at the University of California Medical Center," he told me, but did not give me the definite diagnosis I had hoped for. He was warm and friendly, patiently answered questions, and I had confidence in him.

Barbara's evaluation at the University of California took another two days and was even more thorough. I had a hunch that it was going to be a siege, but I was not prepared for such a molten experience. In those days it took at least five hours to drive to San Francisco. Thank goodness Olga again offered to come along and help. Barbara's first appointment — for a psychometric test — was scheduled for nine in the morning, so we had to stay overnight again. Again she slept in the closet, and we took along her stroller for she still was not walking, and I knew that parking near the hospital would be difficult.

I had never experienced a public clinic. The impersonality of it appalled and intimidated me. As a doctor's daughter I had always had very personal medical attention. Here long lines of people waited in corridors or on hard wooden benches. There was no place to put down a small child to change diapers or take a nap. There was no lunchroom nearby or handy vending machines. After the psychological test we were interviewed by a social worker who filled out impressive forms. Half a dozen residents and interns poked and prodded Barbara at irregular intervals. They asked me questions but never volunteered an answer. I had no way of knowing if one of them was the specialist, Dr. Peter Cohen, we had come to see, for they would come and disappear without bothering to introduce themselves.

Towards the end of the second afternoon, a nurse led us into another small examining room. She said that the professor would be coming to speak with us soon. Barbara looked grubby and felt cranky. She was thoroughly bored with the entire process and with the few toys I had brought from home. She was sitting on the floor, chewing on a tongue depressor when the door opened and a middle-aged, slightly paunchy gentleman came in. "I'm Dr. Cohen," he said as he shook my hand and halfway propped himself against the examining table on which I had been sitting. He was followed by half a dozen men and women in white coats. One or two of them looked faintly familiar. They were the pokers and prodders of yesterday and today. "So that's Barbara," Dr. Cohen said and waved to her from across the room. "Well, mother," he continued. "She will probably never make Phi Beta Kappa, but that will bother her a lot less than it will you."

Beyond that I remember very little. I was too tired and confused to ask many questions. Dr. Cohen had nice eyes and a warm smile, but he appeared hurried. He instructed me to check with a social worker on the way out. She would want to take my address so that we could make future plans. "Regards to Dr. Peck," he said as he left. "And let me see Barbara again in half a year."

I don't believe that the words "mental retardation" were spoken on that occasion. We returned to Dr. Peck's office in Santa Rosa a few weeks later to discuss the results of the University of California evaluation. Again it was summertime and the grandparents were visiting us, so my father volunteered to come along.

When we were all led into the office, the two physicians put their heads together, but Papi pulled out of the huddle, looked at me, and said: "No, no, Doctor. You can tell Lotte too. She's strong. She can handle this." Instinctively he appealed to my courage and thus buffered the news and the hurt of the diagnosis. Barbara was indeed "mentally retarded."

From left: Karen, David, Barbara

Chapter 4

It Feels Like That Time Before

This hurt was bad. Hearing Barbara called retarded hurt like hell — and although I was surrounded by a loving husband, parents, two cute kids and good neighbors I felt alone and bereft — in some corner of my heart even ashamed. The concept of mental retardation had strong, hopeless overtones that had been indelibly imprinted on me by years of societal fear and prejudice. Our chubby, cuddly child was suddenly being relegated to a darkened future.

The pain conjured up devastating experiences from the past that I had tried to put away. Now I was forced to look at them again. I could remember other painful times in my life but they had always disappeared gradually. Would this one too? I didn't see how. But I had to make sure that I would be able to go on. It was a slow process. My busy life as an orderly housewife, mother of three, and occasional substitute teacher did not give me much time to sit and brood.

How did I feel? It's hard to remember. Thoughts and feelings don't stand still. Like the surf at the edge of the sand they advance and retreat, sometimes gently and at other times with stormy force. I can still recall the shock and pain, but forty years later much of it has been healed by feelings of hope, optimism and admiration that have come from knowing Barbara and seeing her grow up. I do remember I felt a little better after my worries about Barbara's development had been replaced by a definite diagnosis, but the problem itself was there — huge and immovable as a rock.

Through three pregnancies I had taken for granted that our children would all be healthy and bright. I could not recall ever knowing anyone who was visibly disabled — certainly not as a schoolmate. I knew about my father's patients but that was different. They had physical illnesses. If any of my college psychology courses mentioned the problem of mental retardation it had gone in one ear and out the other. While I was six months pregnant with Karen, a good friend's first baby was stillborn, but that also was different. I was deeply sad for her, but did not think that this would happen to me. After all, my baby was busily moving around inside me.

The words "mental retardation" shocked and frightened me. I felt sorry for myself, and I prayed as I had not done since those adolescent days in Hitler's Germany that I might wake up one morning and find this was all a bad dream.

I am sure I fit the prototype of the newly wounded mother during that summer of 1955. I must have been in the first of the three stages which professionals of the day assigned to the parents of children with disabilities, and it wouldn't surprise me to find that these three stages are still being taught in some college classes.

First you feel guilty and wonder what you have done wrong to give birth to this child who shatters the dream of the perfect heir and the promise of becoming President of the United States! Next you exchange this period of sorrow and introspection for one of action, which is not necessarily purposeful or coordinated. It is, however, some activity outside of your own head and heart. For some parents this turns into "shopping trips" from one specialist to another in an attempt to exchange the initial diagnosis for something less hurtful. I think I escaped that stage. Partly because I had grown up with basic trust in the physicians in my own family — and now because of the good and caring doctors we had met. We may not have had access to all the diagnostic knowledge and treatments of the nineties, but we were confident that they were trying to help and support us in our efforts to move Barbara towards a more hopeful future.

The third stage frequently involves cooperation with other parents "who have been there," in an effort to locate or establish support programs for our children. Immediate support — right at birth or at the moment of doubt or diagnosis — is sadly not always available but knowledge and information ARE out there. From the midwife, pediatrician or birthing room — from the phone book to the Internet — we are able to find organizations that can help. Parents who have been there themselves, public health nurses and "Early Start" home and school support programs can lessen the pain and worry and disappointment. Talking with someone who has had a similar experience provides a tremendous buffer to new parents' pain and shortens their grieving period. Recently I heard of the father of a newborn with Down Syndrome who was given the number of a local parent group right in the hospital and went directly to the telephone and asked if he could join them.

I'm sure I took the long course. In the beginning I wondered secretly if I might have done something wrong at some time during my pregnancy, but those thoughts dead-ended. I vaguely remembered a slip and fall near the woodstove in our dining nook, but I had bounced lightly and hurt nothing. There had been a minor flu-like illness making its rounds during the early months of my pregnancy. It might have been German Measles, but I had already had it as a child, and was under the impression that I couldn't catch it again. I did still smoke cigarettes at the time (never had inhaled!) but was just discovering that I seemed to need both hands to get my daily chores done. More and more the cigarettes wound up in the ash tray barely touched and the habit just faded away. I thought about alcohol but how could drinking have been the problem? We had some sherry and liquor in the house but used it mostly for guests. Al's post-war stomach was sensitive and my consumption minimal. (We now know better. It *is* harmful for pregnant mothers to drink.) My pregnancy had been smooth and uneventful. Nobody seemed to know of any genetic reason. Then why?

Uncontrollably my thoughts then wandered from the pregnancy to the actual birth process. Had there been a difference in the quality of care during Barbara's birth, and if so, what had it been?

Karen had been delivered by a general practitioner in Fairbanks, and my father had managed to throw his grandfatherly shadow all the way from New York to Alaska. Right from the start Papi took a dim view of my producing a first grandchild in the northern wilderness, and so when I wrote him that our Dr. Weston would be coming to New York for a medical conference, he went to great lengths to meet his young colleague and took him out for lunch to the finest French restaurant he could think of. I suspect they talked about my pregnancy and care and that Dr. Weston felt extra responsible until the day of Karen's birth. I was proud and elated then, with the baby safely out and the feeling rapidly returning to my lower end. Dr. Weston seemed to go on and on with the sewing of my episiotomy. "Just one more stitch," he insisted over my yowls that he was starting to hurt me. "We've got to do a good job here so Lotte's father will be pleased," he said to the nurse, as if he really believed that my father would inspect anything but the actual end product of the delivery.

With David's birth in New York I had the most loving and expert care a woman could expect. Dr. Langstadt was not only a friend of the family, but also an experienced obstetrician who had never lost a baby in fifty years of medical practice. He was doubly supportive because of Al's being overseas, and besides, he knew something he would not let me know. David was in a breech position.

If he were alive today I know he would have leveled with me. During one of my pre-natal exams he prodded and poked my abdomen more vigorously than usual. "Hey! Why are you being so rough today?" I asked him. He gave an excuse (he was actually trying to turn the baby). And when I asked to see the x-ray, my Dad and Dr. Langstadt arranged for the lab in the neighboring hospital to show me a picture of another baby — one that was head down! David however did not cooperate and insisted on being a breech birth. I am sure that today they would have dignified me by making me a partner in their concern.

I labored from early morning until evening, and all during that long, hot June day Dr. Langstadt stayed close by in the hospital, often holding my hand, and even during the tricky last stage of birth he supported me when I insisted I did not want to have any anesthesia.

When I went into labor with my third child, I discovered that deliveries in small rural hospitals in the fifties were a little more haphazard. Fort Bragg physicians were overworked. Some of them lived miles out of town and could not come in for deliveries in the two small, private hospitals until the last minute. Because of the distances involved, they frequently had to cover for one another when babies made unscheduled appearances. There was no physician on duty on a round the clock basis. The evening Barbara went into action, our regular physician was out of town, and there were two elderly nurses on the night shift. It was customary for one of the two to take a nap in the linen room if all was calm. I lay in a regular bed in a six-bed ward and "labored" as efficiently and quietly as I could, all by myself. After all I was an old pro with my third pregnancy and considered myself somewhat of a pioneer in the "Childbirth Without Pain" movement of Dr. Grantley Dick Read. I had read this British gynecologist's book and practiced his new method of exercises and relaxation with both Karen and David and was awake and aware when they were born.

With Barbara I went into heavy labor sometime during the early morning hours. My roommate, who was the proud mother of a day-old boy, had just asked the nurse for a bedpan when I needed to be rolled into the delivery room. That poor woman sat on the throne for about an hour; she claimed she had a permanent ring on her bottom by the time the nurse came back to liberate her. We still joke about it when we run into each other in the grocery store and compare notes on our children.

It took the doctor a while to drive into town, and I think I was holding back from those last almighty thrusts which might have pushed out the baby earlier. In those days we had no fetal monitors with which to check on the baby's heartbeat and oxygen supply. There was no Apgar Scale to score the infant's condition right after birth. Perhaps Barbara did not get enough oxygen during that last stage of birth. We'll never know, but I have always wondered. Such broodings, however, were clearly counterproductive. Dishes and dust cooties piled up and made me feel worse. I put my guilty thoughts and retroactive wondering aside and discovered the healing qualities of movement and work.

In many ways nothing seemed to change in our daily doings after we came home with The Diagnosis. We continued our orderly, busy lives. Karen was now in the first grade and loved reading. David pushed little cars around in the dirt and looked forward to kindergarten. Barbara was almost two. I remember it as my gray period.

We worked mightily. The printshop was an all-consuming effort for Al. He left for work right after breakfast, took a sack lunch, and did not return until time for dinner. I'd have the children all scrubbed and in their bathrobes — ready to tell him of their adventures and accomplishments of the day. Except for Barbara. She had started saying "Mama" and "Dada" when she was a year and a half; not much more speech had developed since then. But she welcomed her daddy with an enchanting smile and body wiggle as she sat propped up against the refrigerator, waving her arms ecstatically. He gave her a full share of his attention and included her in the bedtime story and tucking-in ceremony with her own special piggy-back ride into bed.

On many evenings Al took a nap after dinner and returned to his shop for several more hours. And even though his work ethic (to deliver orders to his customers as promised) was overwhelming, we were so broke. He put in a full day on Saturdays and several hours of work on many a Sunday too. I began to wait anxiously for his return at supper time, for if he came loaded down with boxes, it meant hours of folding, collating, or putting stamps on business envelopes. This "women's handwork" of the printing trade, as it was then called, wasn't bad when we did it together, but it was deadly dull on lonesome evenings when Al had returned to his shop. We had no television then, so I listened to the radio or played reams of records and worried about Barbara.

She was certainly making progress all the time. Our neighbors could see it and told me so. I entered each developmental milestone in her small blue health record: "First tooth at five months; sat unsupported at ten months; began to grab things with hands at twelve months." By the time we celebrated her second birthday and the

Christmas of 1955 she had begun to crawl and was playing with her new peg toy. She was talented in other ways too. She had learned to feed herself with a spoon and participated proudly in potty training. When we went on an occasional family picnic or a hike with friends, Al patiently carried Barbara on his broad shoulders while other kids her age toddled around under their own steam.

With all of his great love and warmth and patience, Al could not yet face up squarely to his little girl's problems. Stubbornly he continued to quarrel with the dour predictions of the doctors, and I had a hard time discussing her future with him. One evening a good friend came for supper. Ed was the father of the young man from whom Al took over the printshop, and was a teacher of printing and other industrial arts subjects at our high school. The conversation got around to education in general and to our youngest daughter's educational future in particular. I wondered what sort of practical courses a child like ours could take and asked Ed about the vocational offerings of Fort Bragg High School. "What has your experience with such students been, Ed?" Again Al became angry. Any child, given quality teaching by patient teachers could learn any academic subject, he maintained. He really believed that Barbara might be able to learn mathematics and physics if only we tried hard enough. At the end of that debate I felt defeated.

Now I know Al was more right than wrong. I often quote a passage from a speech given in 1977 by my chief mentor, Dr. Gunnar Dybwad, Emeritus Professor of Human Development, Brandeis University — a giant in the parent movement nationally and worldwide — in which he said:

"In dealing with the problem of human growth and development one should never say 'never'—there is always change, the dynamics of which so far have not become clear to scientific exploration—no one can predict as a human being is born where the limits of that person's growth and development will be. I reject and resent the arrogance of bureaucratic and professional workers who predetermine another human being's potential."

Many other times he has said that it's not that our sons and daughters with cognitive problems cannot learn, but that we need to learn better how to teach. We *have* made strides in that direction and I have become a believer in his credo.

Al and I made no bones about Barbara's diagnosis, but we seldom talked with our friends and neighbors about our worries, and I had not yet actually met fellow parents. It was not until later that Dodie Scott was to become my most significant partner.

If our friends thought of Barbara as different they did not tell us then. They too seemed to be looking for the positive. We included her in all our outings, and everyone accepted her as one of the kids. The friends with whom we socialized and exchanged baby-sitting were tremendously helpful and generous, especially Edith Hall, the wife of our family doctor. At the end of a baby sitting afternoon I could relax over a cup of coffee and air my worries without getting blasted and we'd compare notes on the children's interactions and the babies' bowel movements. Often Edith would tell me about Barbara's newest accomplishments. She had held a toy or almost turned from her back to her stomach. In spite of the demands of her own three, she managed to spend time on her very own mobility program for Barbara.

It worked both ways. I did the same for her and at the time didn't think of it as a "service." It was the way neighborliness worked in a small town, and I now realize what a blessing it was then and how different it is now for many families. So many parents both work; so many mothers are single. I now rank RESPITE at the head of my list of priorities as an essential support for families who have children with special developmental needs.

Our family had the additional benefit of three grandparents who were intensely concerned and involved — each in their own way. During the winter we wrote to them regularly. Letter writing was my department and Al would comment "You do write good letters, dear," as he signed them at breakfast. In the summer Nana, Papi and Mud, Al's mom, came to Fort Bragg to stay for several weeks. Interestingly enough their attitudes towards Barbara and our family's problem differed sharply. My father's was naturally clinical. From time to time he would come up with a new thought or theory that he had read about or discussed with his sister who was also a physician. He'd ask me to check it out with our doctor. "Has Barbara had a thyroid test?" he wondered, and I reported back to him when I found out. Overall, though, he could find no fault with our doctors' diagnosis and recommendations. He thought they were doing a thorough, careful job and I am still impressed today when I look over their reports of many years ago.

My mother seemed to accept Barbara quite matter-of-factly. During her many years as a visiting grandma she became the official recorder of the children's growth and development, for she came loaded with film. Papi used to accuse her of "shooting from the hip," and often she did cut off a head or two. My own camera stayed shelved during most of these years. Nana intuitively understood that she could be as firm and as strict with Barbara as she had been with Karen and David, and once Barbara was able to get around on her own, she had no trouble taking care of her. After my father died and she moved from New York to an apartment here in town, she willingly looked after Barbara whenever we asked her to, until her own health began to fail.

Al's mother, Grandma Mud, showed her love for her youngest grandchild in a different way. She never did seem to overcome her feelings of hurt and sorrow for us and for Barbara. Even years later when she too lived in Fort Bragg, she loved Barbara to a fault. We patiently tried to explain that we wanted her to treat Barbara like any other little girl. Barbara also had to learn limits. "Please don't let her have any candy when she visits you!" we'd plead. "She's too chubby now and it'll ruin her teeth."

Mud's invariable refrain would be, "Oh, let her — she enjoys it so," with pity in her voice. Many years later, when Barbara had grown into a teenager, I overheard Mud say to an elderly friend: "Yes, isn't she pretty? Too bad she is so sick." Inwardly I groaned about our failure to convince her that Barbara's slowness and special developmental needs called for a positive approach and that she was slow in learning some things but she certainly was not sick. There is a book on my shelf written by a fellow mother of a child with a disability. Sandra Kaufman's book is called *Retarded ISN'T Stupid, Mom!* — a direct quote from her daughter.

During the early years of Barbara's life, Karen and David were the healing ingredients in our recovery process. We watched them move and grow apace, and they kept us all busy with Blue Birds, Cub Scouts, Sunday School and Open Houses at the elementary school. Regardless of how busy Al was, he took the time to take part in any and all gatherings that required the presence of parents. He was the one who loaded the stroller into the trunk of the car, packed Barbara on his back, or bundled three sleepy children from car to bed after we had spent an evening visiting or square dancing. Karen and David seemed to take their little sister pretty much for granted during those early years. They were interested enough to report on her progress and applaud her efforts, but when she violated their territorial rights (all three shared one bedroom and a large toy box), they protested loudly. Recognition of their own troubled feelings as siblings of Barbara had not yet surfaced in our consciousness. We know better now.

The first report from the University of California Clinic states "the mother feels that the child is making constant improvement." I firmly believe this was the key to Barbara's progress. We thought she would and so she did. Al especially continued to challenge her with high expectations, and — slowly but surely — she lived up to them and proved him right.

Luckily, I did not rush to the library to read everything and anything I could find as I had done during David's TB scare. The card index renderings on "mental deficiency" in a small town library of the fifties would have been sparse and depressing. There were no books then like Bob Perske's *Hope For The Families; New Directions for Parents of Persons with Retardation or Other Disabilities,* which might have helped us work through our fears. Besides, a part of me — influenced by Al — was still hiding behind the thin veil of hope that Barbara's problem would turn out to be the kind of slow learning one can remedy with extra tutoring. Perhaps hers would be like my little brother Henry's slow start in school. I remembered how he had blossomed thanks to Nana's patient daily help with homework.

My gray period burst into furious red on the day a little parcel arrived in the mail. At first I didn't even recognize the name of the sender. Then I remembered. She was a woman I had met while sitting on one of those brown wooden benches at the University of California Clinic several months before. She was sending me Dale Evans Rogers' book, *Angel Unaware,* with best wishes for our family. One look at the jacket blurb and I was indignant. How could it have been so obvious to her that our child had mental retardation? The Rogerses' baby had died. They viewed her as a special gift from heaven and a very temporary visitor on earth. How could this woman put our robust, rosy-cheeked Barbara into the same bag with the Rogerses' slowly fading "angel"? But, she had made the connection, and that's what hurt.

It was both a bad shock and a good shock. For the first time I was able to see Barbara as others saw her. I could recognize the words "mental retardation" as the all-encompassing concept that it is to most people, which wipes out individual differences in their eyes and hopes in the hearts of parents. To the world out there, our child would be "different" and thus relegated to a segregated future. That was the red fighting flag. Our hopes see-sawed along for the rest of that year, and we measured Barbara's smallest progress with pride, but my thoughts were beginning to run far ahead. I wanted to plan and protect her years into the future. Should we try putting her into a private nursery school? Would they let her into kindergarten? How about love and marriage? Al steadfastly maintained that she was outgrowing her problem, and now we realize that we were both right and that Barbara landed somewhere between his stubborn positive presumptions and my activist anxieties.

In the spring of 1956, when she was two years and four months old, she started to walk. It happened at Edith and Lloyd Hall's house while I was out of town with David and Karen. We stopped at Al's shop on our way home. "Better go pick up Barbara right away," he said, unable to contain his excitement. "They have a surprise for you." The surprise was Barbara. Edith and Kris, their six-year old had let go of her hands and helped her reach this monumental milestone. She was actually walking alone. It was a funny-looking walk, but we thought it was beautiful. There she stood, straddle-legged, both hands gripping the straps on her denim overalls for dear life, her tongue sticking out between her lips. The several steps she took towards us were wobbly, but she was proud as punch.

So Barbara was able to walk into the office of the University of California professor when we returned for our one-year appointment. "Dr. Cohen would like you to bring your husband and Barbara's siblings if at all possible," the secretary had said. "Doctor likes to talk with the whole family."

It was a much more pleasant visit than the one a year before. Having the whole family together made it seem almost like an outing. Dr. Cohen's private office was warm and comfortable, and we hardly had to wait at all. Al and I went in first with Barbara, and Al was finally able to meet the doctor about whom I had spoken so much. Dr. Cohen examined Barbara briefly and noted her progress. Then Al and I had a chance to air our different expectations.

"No!" Dr. Cohen said honestly. "This will *not* go away. She will not outgrow the problem, but in your good family you can expect to see her develop. Let me see her again later, and now I would also like to talk with Karen and David." He was excellent with our two older children, now five and seven years old. The crux of his message was, "Help your small sister with all the things that you know how to do, but don't help her too much. Let her try. Don't do things for her!" On that day he cut them in as partners on our family team, and we began to learn from each other — all five of us.

"Barbara not sucking my thumb anymore
— that's making Chas Happy!"

Chapter 5

We Were Not Alone

We were not alone with our trouble but didn't yet know it — back in 1956. Except for our family's reliance on our medical support team we still thought we should take the "stiff upper lip" position and solve our problems by ourselves. We were unaware there was a budding movement afoot in the world. Soon after World War II parents of children with developmental special needs erupted into action. It happened on different continents and in many different countries. These stubborn, belligerent, constructive efforts grew from parents' mutual concern about their children and their own need for support into a force for change — the *Parent Movement.*

It was an uphill struggle. One mother in Philadelphia decided to place an ad in the paper to ask if another parent with a child like her own might contact her. The paper refused to run the ad because "this was too shamefully embarrassing."

To my knowledge sociologists have never come up with a reason for this movement out of the closet on behalf of our children. Perhaps it was because the world war with its huge loss of human life had triggered a heightened awareness of its value.

Inadvertently our family benefited from this, for the parent movement had already come to Fort Bragg before Barbara was born.

Several women had observed children with noticeable disabilities in the stores and on the streets always accompanied by their mothers, when other children were in school. In a small town one notices such things. What happened to these children in our town? "Not much" was the answer, and a few phone calls and cups of coffee later, they had pooled their talents and energies and formed a group. Some of these women had moved to Fort Bragg with their husbands who worked in our large lumber mill. They had experience in teaching, social work, occupational therapy or nursing. Others were homemakers.

They determined that the mothers of these children needed some relief time and hired a woman to sit and play with the children three mornings a week in a local church for fifty cents an hour. "We really intended this service as nothing more than respite for the parents," Josephine Wheeler, the founding president told me. "We certainly didn't believe that they were capable of learning."

The program had to be discontinued when the salaried person moved away, but under Jo's leadership the Parents and Friends of Retarded Children was duly incorporated in 1955 and became one of the first such parent organizations in the state of California.

Some of the founding members are still alive. Josephine is now in a nursing home and doesn't remember much, but when I visit her she always asks, "And how is Barbara?" Once when I remarked to one of the nurses that Jo had founded the local parent organization she said: "Did *I* do *that?*"

Al and I weren't ready for this yet. I vaguely remember reading small newspaper notices of their meetings in the boiler room of one of the schools but had no intention of attending them. I think it was a mixture of denial and even shame. We had our own small circle of friends and neighbors, and my activities such as PTA and volunteer swim teaching seemed still to be focused on the hope for a "normal" future for Barbara. Virginia was one member of the group who was and has remained a stalwart lifelong friend and even she refrained from urging me to join them. One did not easily inflict such a painful invitation on a friend.

The first task of the early parent associations was to identify the developmental special needs of their children. They felt they needed to describe what was wrong before they could apply pressure for needed programs and services. Now we know that all children have strong and weak suits. We can measure and plot the high and low points on a developmental profile and then build bridges to strengthen the overall functioning of every child. We can often zero in on each person's developmental special need without hanging a stigmatizing, permanent label around his or her neck.

I couldn't have explained any of this back in 1956. Our family acted on hunches. Barbara's strong suits had to do with hunger and elimination. She fed herself by hand or by spoon at about the same time and with the same messy eagerness of children her age. Toilet training also proceeded on schedule. Because we cheered successes and didn't make a big deal about messes, she learned these skills proudly and well. Her speech and gross motor coordination, however, were noticeably slow. Were she a toddler today she could benefit tremendously from extra help in these areas.

I used to pray that Barbara would learn to talk. Our family is an articulate bunch, and the prospect of establishing a communicating relationship without speech seemed overwhelmingly difficult. Barbara's little blue medical record book states that she said "Mama" and "Dada" when she was nineteen months old and that she was able to play "pattycake" about the same time. The fact that she was able to recognize members of our family and others who were close friends was evident from the gleeful expression on her face and an overall body wiggle which is a language in itself.

We listened patiently to Barbara's every monosyllable. "Guess what Barbara said today!" became standard reporting procedure, and one day she really surprised me. She was walking by then, so she must have been about two and a half years old. She picked up a penny from the floor in the grocery store and brought it to me. "Mummy, money!" she said, clearly differentiating between the two middle consonants. This was more than a person's name or an object word repeated. She had made a statement that described a concept, and that was exciting. We aren't a money-oriented family, so we were amazed to discover our youngest daughter's early financial bent! Her new word was especially encouraging because we knew that if she could say two words that reached outside of her immediate family constellation, she would learn other concepts in time.

So we bumbled along with our stimulation program, unplanned and disorganized as it was. When Karen and David were little, we had seldom allowed them to stay up late. We believed in regular bedtime hours and plenty of sleep, but Barbara seemed to brighten with excitement and less routine. She was animated instead of crabby on the morning after. So the stroller was put into the back of the car more and more often, as PTA potlucks, school recitals and friendly picnics involved our family.

Today I look at other parents who have much more seriously disabled sons and daughters than Barbara, and marvel at their patience and energy as I read the accounts of their lives. I'm not sure I could have functioned against such odds.

It was a good thing Barbara liked riding in cars, for to this day a steady stomach, strong spine, and patient backside are prerequisites for getting from Fort Bragg to anywhere else, and to be a parent advocate still requires many crooked miles.

Karen had been a wiggle worm from the beginning — always trying to squirm out of her car seat and wanting to know, "When do we get there? How much longer is it?" David was the exact opposite. As long as the wheels were turning he was happy and wide-eyed. I hoped that this wasn't a male characteristic and it was not. Barbara also rode happily wherever we took her. In fact, both Karen and I required many more service station pit stops than she did.

Other aspects of family outings, however, weren't necessarily smooth and easy. Barbara was fearful. She used to cry out in panic at the sudden dimming of lights in an auditorium or theater, and when she met a friend downtown who was a favorite, she expressed her delight in strange ways. She pummeled the person with her fists, screeched, and threw herself on the sidewalk. We didn't understand why she did this. Was the reason that the words of joy and recognition would not come out? It was embarrassing and people told us that they wondered if she would ever learn to behave like other children.

Once a friendly fireman in San Francisco showed our children his big red engine. As a special treat he rang the bell for them. The sound reverberated in the tiny station house. Barbara screamed in terror and we had to calm her and thank him at the same time. But gradually she got used to most of the strange sights and sounds of her environment and learned to act more appropriately. Her greatest early triumph occurred during a Saturday children's matinee at the local movie theater.

She won the drawing for the big prize — a bicycle. Karen and David reported how well she handled the situation. They called her name and asked her to come up on stage to accept the prize. She climbed the steps slowly. "Is your name Barbara Moise?" asked the manager. She nodded and beamed. "Would you like to say something?"

"Thank you," she said clearly, and everyone applauded.

She never learned to ride that bike, but it remained in her possession for years. She took great pride in owning it, and from time to time she wheeled it out of the shed and pushed it around our house. Al spent many hours trying to teach her how to ride, but even with training wheels she didn't seem to have the balance and coordination for the rough and bumpy ground around our house.

When Barbara occasionally mentions that bike, I realize much was missing in her early gross motor development program. We knew that our baby was lying on her back far too long and that she was sitting still too patiently. But it took endless hours to hold her in a standing position or to encourage her to take a step. There didn't seem to be enough hours in the day. I probably wasn't patient enough and tended to be a somewhat compulsively neat housewife. A neat house was important to me, whereas Edith, at whose house Barbara had taken those first solo steps, could overlook housework and work with Barbara in spite of disorder.

The County Public Health doctor came to small rural communities like ours at intervals and held well baby clinics in the Veterans' Memorial Building. Parents took their small children there for required shots and immunizations. Dr. Kroeger was a bit brusque, but kind. "She has flat feet," he said and recommended an orthopedist — the nearest one in the county seat fifty-five crooked miles over the

41

coast range. "Congenital flat fleet," was that doctor's diagnosis, and added "Better keep her in high top boots with arches and steel shafts." That was the extent of his advice and added another puzzle rather than solution to her care.

There was a shoemaker in our town who specialized in boots for loggers. We would draw around Barbara's feet on a piece of paper and Mr. Makela sent the picture to a shoemaker in Hong Kong with further instructions on the type of heel, and kind and color of leather. I treasure my correspondence with this polite gentleman who would announce the completion of the shoes: "Our competent workingman has used the finest workmanship and best sort of leather... please be reminded that you will receive her shoes with content and happiness. You and Miss Barbara will be extremely pleased with our superior craftsmanship..." and then would come a request for payment and another letter announcing that the shoes had been shipped by sea mail. Quite a trip.

Nobody quite realized how important it would be for her future mobility to strengthen specific muscles and to encourage balance and coordination. The skills and support of a physiotherapist or adaptive recreation therapist would have helped us immensely in structuring our program for Barbara's motor development.

It saddens me now when I look at our awkward, uncoordinated and often fearful daughter and think of the skills she might have learned. She might have learned to ride that bike, to climb up and down steep places, and to get on and off escalators. There is little doubt in my mind we could have taught her to bridge more of the gaps in her coordination, because she loosens up and is ecstatically happy when she dances and in the water she relaxes and swims with confidence.

Later on, when I became a special education teacher, I blundered into physical activities for our students as the need for them crossed my inexperienced mind. Our schoolhouse was poorly insulated and icy cold on winter mornings, so it made sense to warm up with exercises. Music seemed to support movement, so we danced. I was a Red Cross Water Safety Instructor — totally convinced that swimming is good for everybody. Our small town had a heated indoor pool, so we taught swimming. It all just happened — and it happened to be exactly what was needed.

Barbara asks me occasionally why she cannot drive a car. We talk about it, and I try to help her face the reality of her physical limitations. I remind her of her aunt who never learned to ride a bike or drive a car and our neighbor who can't swim. It is sad for her and for us, but it is as real as a physical condition that puts others in wheelchairs. In hope of consoling her, I tell Barbara about my own awkward attempts at skating and skiing when I was younger and how I decided to give up these activities. Still, the confession of my own failures is small consolation in our mobile, motorized world, and we find it difficult to strike a fine balance between encouraging her to try and discouraging unrealistic expectations.

Our early stimulation program for our little girl continued to be haphazard as we worked with her, four ways towards the middle.

I taught her to recognize colors from a Hudson Bay blanket. Every morning when she helped me make our double bed, we played games with the bright red, green, black and yellow stripes. "Show me the red! Is this green?" I would say, as I pointed to the wrong color over and over, until she knew and was able to identify colors and say the words.

Phonograph records contributed greatly to the noise level at our house, and they became a valued teaching device. When the children were little, Al would wake us all up with his favorite startlers — bagpipes, drumbeats, and jazz. Later Al and I were drowned out by our adolescent children's even noisier rock and country and western discs. Barbara loved music and rhythm. Singing along seemed to help new words come out. She surprised us in being smarter than her sister Karen in catching onto the workings of the automatic record player. She handled it intelligently and carefully. Karen instinctively capitalized on this discovery to build up Barbara's self-confidence. "Come here a minute, Barb! I can't start this thing," she would say, and Barbara would hurry over, push the right button, and make it play. Here was another puzzle in the unevenness of Barbara's development: if she could do this, why not something else?

Our favorite game at bedtime became "Hide the Thimble." It was Al's idea that it might sharpen Barbara's powers of observation and perception. She had outgrown a slight problem with her eyes not tracking together when she was a baby. Now it was more a problem of seeing what was right in front of her nose. So we hid the thimble all over our house, and Karen and David eagerly coached her in the right direction as she toddled from room to room in her bathrobe. "You're cold, Barb, icy cold. Now you're getting warmer. Hot! Hot! You *found* it!" and in the process she learned about up and down, in front of and behind, and under and over — all essential concepts that other children learn without prompting.

During these first five years of Barbara's life, we were still hoping the public schools would provide whatever special education programs she would need. In the meantime, though, it seemed like a good idea to give her extra help to get ready for school. Karen and David had been busy enough without nursery school, but Barbara needed more stimulation than we could give her at home. When she was four, we enrolled her in a private nursery school along with three little neighbor girls, and it felt comfortably "normal" to me to be taking turns in the carpool.

It was through PTA work that I first recognized the pioneering efforts of our small local group of parents of children with developmental needs. I attended a district meeting at which the featured speaker was the president of the California Parent Teacher Association. She was a wise and wonderful woman who spoke eloquently of special education programs for children who were "mentally retarded." She told us about certain new sections of the 1956 State of California Education Code which mandated that school districts of a certain size provide classes for the "educably mentally retarded."

As the questions from the audience bounced back and forth over my head, I heard definitions of "educable" versus "trainable" students with mental retardation based on IQ points and cut-offs. When they weren't talking about these children as "educable" or "trainable," they seemed to be referring to them as "Point I" or "Point II." All of this sounded as confusing as a new language to me, but I soon found out that Points I and II were the tail ends of four-digit numbers designating sections of the state education code. For many years California youngsters with special developmental needs were labeled as Point I and Point II. Gradually our language has evolved. It has become a sensitive issue for discussion as many of our sons and daughters have grown up to resent and protest these categorical labels and have been instrumental in changing them.

That meeting changed my life. I met my first fellow parent. As we moved through the buffet lunch line I found myself talking to a woman from Fort Bragg whom I had never met before. She had driven over with her teenaged daughter. The girl was strangely quiet as her mother talked about her anxiously. It seemed that nothing was happening for her child in our school district in spite of the new state mandates. Helen had attended regular classes when she was a little girl, but she had withdrawn into silence and was currently excluded from public school. Her mother, in the hope that something could be done for Helen, had recently joined a local group of other parents who had "retarded" children.

That gave me the push I needed. Sometime after this encounter I attended a meeting of this group, Parents and Friends of Retarded Children, for the first time. They met in the basement of the junior high school near the boiler room. I still felt uncomfortable about joining their shoestring operation in such a nonprestigious location. It felt *underground* and I was far from ready to meet the challenge of being part of a pioneering movement. I simply wanted to find out more about our Barbara's chances for a school program.

Several older women in the group stood out from the rest. Mary Wilbur was a robust woman who had long ago raised her own family. She was presently fostering two children in her home. One of her little girls was on leave from a Northern California State Institution. Penny had no speech. She was a tiny, dwarflike creature who had to use her entire body to express anything she wanted to say. Her foster mother, though, had lots to say and energy to burn. Mary and I co-organized picnics and outings for our families that summer, and while we herded children and swapped recipes, she somehow helped me face certain unpleasant realities about our nonexistent service system. She not only complained loud and clear about the uncooperative attitude of Penny's social worker, but she also stood her ground on behalf of the child. Some of that must have rubbed off on me. She knew the ropes and gave me ideas.

Imbie Wirtnen was a retired teacher who was slightly handicapped herself by a limp due to a congenital hip condition. A pretty, gentle woman, she had the gift of diffusing anxiety with a twinkle and an anecdote. Even though Imbie was unmarried and childless, her motherly warmth embraced all children. Her neat home contained a toy box full of surprises, which attracted neighbor children by the dozen. Barbara loved to visit her, and we went often for advice and moral support. When the parent group first organized the part-time childcare service, she had been a faithful and effective volunteer. She was still in there pitching when I first joined the group.

The third member of the troika was Ellen Taylor, another retired teacher. For years she had taught a mixed bag of children in a small logging camp schoolhouse in the woods. Ellen was one of a breed of pioneer women that is now almost extinct, and she had practiced her profession undaunted by distance, weather, or individual differences.

There was one mother in this core group who taught me about the wounds some parents retain even years after the initial diagnosis. When I first met her she was patiently and efficiently working as volunteer treasurer of the organization, but hardly a meeting went by that she did not talk about the unfeeling way in which she had first received the diagnosis of her daughter's condition. She had taken her pretty baby to a large teaching hospital in San Francisco for an examination. "A young resident put her back into my lap," she told us. "He almost threw her. And he hardly looked at me. And then he said, 'Sorry, Ma'am, but I think you should place her in the state hospital right away. She'll never be more than a vegetable.' Then he left."

She and her husband and their baby moved to our small town soon afterwards. She remembered the warm concern of strangers whom she met on the street and in the stores, but it was frequently and bluntly expressed, "You're not going to keep her at home? There must be places for children like this." She painfully remembered what that doctor had said, and now joined the other women in their efforts to create a place for her little girl close to home.

I, too, began to feel involved with their hopes and frustrations. Their aspirations became my own. I came to the realization that I had to narrow my activities from the PTA, with its goals of improving the quality of education for all children, to the more specialized and urgent needs of Barbara.

Soon after I joined the association — sometime in 1957 or 1958 — we received a couple of shocks in short succession. We were now aware of the legislation which mandated special classes for children with mental retardation. Because I was a substitute teacher for the public schools and knew the district superintendent, I was sent forth to tackle him on the matter of the new mandate. We liked each other, and had campaigned on the same side of the political fence. "How about a special class for those of our children who fit the Point I category?" I asked him, trying to impress him with my savvy.

"I want to be frank with you, Lotte," he replied thoughtfully, leaning back in his chair. "The way I feel about retarded children is that if they can maintain themselves in the regular classroom — fine and dandy. If not they should be in an institution." To leave no room for doubt, he added, "No. Our district does not foresee starting a Point I class in the near future." And that was that.

His refusal to cooperate did not propel us into instant action. We were still afraid. About that time — at a statewide meeting — I met a man who was president of another local parent association in a small town. He was organizing a lawsuit against his school district for noncompliance with the new mandate. "I think you're making a mistake," I told him. "In our association we believe in gentle persuasion." This parent spoke forcefully of his son's *right* to an education, and I was appalled by his militancy. "My husband owns a small business, and besides, he's president of the Chamber of Commerce. We simply can't afford to be rebels and radicals." Yes, we were still timid and afraid.

The second time the sky fell in, it was on *my* head. It happened in the office of the elementary school principal, when I took Barbara to an appointment with the school psychologist. We still hoped that she might be able to attend regular kindergarten. "Perhaps they will be able to hold her over for a second year," her nursery school teacher had suggested. She was a retired teacher and had heard of such cases. Here was another straw of hope! If Barbara could spend two years in kindergarten she'd be almost eight, and eight was the suggested starting age for special public school classes. This theory was based on the ratio of calendar age to "mental age" resulting from the psychological testing. We *have* come a long way since then with our current emphasis on Early Start programs.

Barbara was wiggly and vague as I watched her "play games" with the psychologist. They permitted me to be in the room with her for reassurance. I had given psychometric tests myself. I was familiar with this one and could tell that she was doing miserably. The verdict was "No. Barbara is not nearly mature enough for kindergarten." And then the ultimate misery. "Hasn't anybody ever told you that she is Point II?"

It was then that our group began to think of trying to create our own school. It wasn't a totally original idea. Other parents, in other states and other countries, were starting private schools, but it seemed like a terrifying thought to attempt it outside of the public school system. The board pointed their fingers at me as possible teacher because I had the degree from Columbia University and a California teaching credential. We jointly decided that our school, though parent run, would be as good as any public school. For me it meant I would have to get a special education credential, but how?

We discussed it in the group and I talked about it with Al. When I mentioned it to Dr. Cohen, he asked, "Must you do it, Mother? Isn't there anyone else who could do it?" In his wisdom he foresaw the enormous energy such a venture would take, and he was probably considering how it might affect Karen and Barbara.

An education professor from the State College at San Francisco was much more encouraging. Dr. George McCabe had been teaching an evening extension course on counseling and guidance in Fort Bragg. On rainy winter nights it required staying overnight, and occasionally members of his class met informally for coffee and further talk. So Dr. McCabe knew about our family's concerns and I felt free to ask his advice about returning to school. I had a valid California secondary school credential and had just completed a couple of extension courses for an elementary credential. What else would I need? How much time would be required away from home? How much would it cost? What did he think of a mother teaching her own child?

In a long, thoughtful letter he replied, "Why not, Lotte? Barbara is lucky that you have the kind of background which will make it relatively easy for you to get the credential — and we'll help all we can at this end." He introduced me to Professor Jerome Rothstein, who gave me further information. It would take twenty-four additional units for a special credential, but I did not need to take them all at once. A six-week summer workshop, with philosophy, methods, curriculum, crafts, and classroom observation all rolled into one, would give me a special credential "on postponement of requirements," and I could take the rest in drips and drabs. Looking back on it now, it seems like a bootleg process, but it worked. One time after we had actually begun the school I asked him what he wanted from me in the way of reports or anecdotal records. His answer was: "Just let me know from time to time that you're still doing it."

It was Dr. Rothstein who suggested that I apply for a fellowship from the Crown Zellerbach Foundation, and when I received it, Al and I could eliminate one of our worries. We'd be able to pay our baby-sitters for the summer as well as my room and board in San Francisco. Our parent group pledged their full moral support. With my credential I could be the qualified teacher, and as soon as we felt ready, we would begin a class.

Only one good friend had doubts about my venture and the honesty to voice them to me. "Why do you want to put so much energy into working with the retarded, when you have so much to offer normal children?"

And what about Karen and David? They were now ten and eight — not old enough to venture forth on activities alone. How would they survive six precious summer vacation weeks with only a weekend mother? Al and I decided to call a family conference. We explained that Sylvia and Eileen would be their baby-sitters. Though these women probably couldn't organize many beach trips and picnics, since neither of them knew how to drive, they would be good cooks and storytellers. And our friends would include them in their outings. I'd come home every Friday evening and stay until Sunday night. This would give me time to write up the week's menu, shop for food and re-group the forces. "What do you think, children?" They thought. Karen spoke first. "Okay, Mom, if it's going to help Barbara get a class, okay." David nodded in agreement. We were on our way.

Barbara with the bike she won but never learned how to ride

Chapter 6

Teacher Goes To School

We were unaware of it then, but our family was embarking on a new way of life that summer of 1959. Gone forever was my resolve that I would not work full time until we had raised our children. I would have to leave home for parts of the next four summers to complete the special education credential. I was becoming increasingly busy with part time substituting and community activities, while trying to love, please, and care for one husband, three children, and an assorted number of dogs, cats, lambs, turtles, a horse and a duck.

Al was still putting in endless evening and weekend hours to build up his printing business. David and Karen took part in Sunday school, Blue Birds and Cub Scouts in addition to stretching their minds with books and testing their muscles with stilts, bikes, horses and swimming. As a family we celebrated every conceivable holiday on the calendar, and we all brought home our friends for fun and meals. At times our house resembled a youth hostel.

From time to time the children complained. "We never go anywhere," David wailed.

"Nancy's parents took her camping," Karen informed us. "Dad works all the time — and now you too, Mom." That's when we should have been more sensitive to their feelings. We were proud of them for being helpful and on the surface understanding, but did not listen carefully to the hurt inside. Later, when they were able to look back at their

51

childhood, they gave Al and me passing grades as parents. True, David has never forgiven us for selling the vintage Rolls Royce without consulting him when he was five. And more than once Karen accused me of being neat and clean to the point of "anal compulsion" because I insisted that she tidy up her messy room. "But we always knew your were there," they both said. Somehow we must have managed to make up for the quick pace of our lives with warmth and love.

We survived the separation of my first summer away. In fact it turned out to be a launching pad for us all. I learned to overcome my fear of arts and crafts. I knew well why I was so afraid of it. A grouchy bear of a first grade teacher in Germany had spoiled it for me for life, or so I thought. As the youngest child in her class, my fingers were clumsier than those of the others — and she had rubbed it in. Whether it was sewing on a button, crocheting a potholder, or drawing a vase, she had made me feel ashamed of the results. Years later I still felt inept. My friend, Virginia, who was an occupational therapist, gave me the encouragement I needed. "Heavens, Lotte," she burst out, "if a kindergartner can learn to do those things, you can too!" So, to my surprise, I discovered that I wasn't all thumbs after all. When I began to turn out creditable cutting, pasting, finger painting and clay projects, my family's appreciation was touching. I found out how important it is, especially after experiencing failure, to receive praise and to be reinforced for small successes. Al hung my school painting in the bathroom to cover a hole in the paneling. Karen argued with David over who could put my blue cardboard wastebasket in their room. I was pleased and proud.

Al and the children also learned much that summer. On weekends I came home full of descriptions of our class trips and observations, and told them all about current theories, methods and nomenclatures. Then the language of special education began to cause us anxiety. Sometime earlier we had jointly decided that Barbara should not constantly have to hear the words "mental retardation." Instinctively, we shrank from wounding her with that term, but to spell m-e-n-t-a-l r-e-t-a-r-d-a-t-i-o-n at the supper table was obviously awkward, even for Papa the Printer and Super Speller.

At the time it was clearly necessary to describe and define our children's special needs precisely. That's the only way we were able to get anywhere with the legislators and educators whom we were belaboring for programs. "But," we would add whenever we described the special conditions of mental retardation, "our children are more like other children than they are different." We believed it and were prepared to prove it by talking of our sons' and daughters' warmth and affection, their loyalty and love, their recognition of old friends and familiar tunes, and the practical skills they were learning from pioneer programs. We wanted it clearly understood that their problem of mental retardation was secondary to their humanness.

Every Friday evening after I drove home from San Francisco State after five days of total immersion in mental retardation theory and five introspective hours alone on the road, I was struck anew with Barbara's solid membership status in our family. She laughed and cried, she hugged and socked her sister and brother, she smiled and pouted. Above all, she was our child, our youngest child, and we loved her.

In spite of all this, the trend of bandying labels about infected our family. So much of our time and energy went into thoughts about Barbara that we seemed unable to shield her from the words. Many years later she shamed us with her own protest. We were talking about one of her "retarded" classmates. "I *hate* that word!" she said.

I shall never forget one landmark summer day in 1959. Our class went on a field trip to visit Sonoma State Hospital, which at the time housed more than four thousand "patients" as they were at the time referred to, with mental retardation. An impressive array of administrators, physicians, psychologists, and top level ward personnel faced the students from behind a long table on the platform in the auditorium.

"Doctor so-and-so will now present the first patient. This is a thirty-three-year-old white, mongoloid female..." droned the voice, as a woman slowly approached the center of the platform facing the audience. "Now, Mary, will you tell me..." the doctor continued in a kindly, but condescending tone, concluding with "Thank you,

Mary," before he went on to the clinical description of the next case. The residents we saw looked content enough. No doubt they were glad to be excused from work or to get away from the routine of ward living. We took copious notes and asked questions of the VIPs lined up before us. There were to be no visits to the wards.

By chance one of the psychologists on the platform turned out to be someone I knew. "Wouldn't you like to see where these people live?" she asked and I jumped at the chance. We skipped lunch so that she could give me a quick tour. My impressions of that tour have since become blurry except for two of the "cottages," as the wards were called. I remember the outdoor play area of one of them that housed crowds of young men who appeared to have no major visible disabilities. The entire area was enclosed with a wire fence — the top as well as the sides — giving it the appearance of a bird cage in a zoo. Symbolically, this eliminated all possibility of flight!

And I remembered well into weeks of restless sleep the "cottage" where seventy little girls lived. All very much like our six-year-old Barbara at home. All trying to touch as they crowded and pushed and stumbled around me, vying for a hug or a word. All calling me "Mama" in their yearning for affection.

I saw our child, lovingly tucked into bed by her parents, surrounded by stuffed animals and crowded by favorite dolls. On that day I knew with overwhelming certainty we were lucky to be able to keep Barbara at home and that she would grow and develop in our family rather than wither in a warehouse. I now had a commitment, a direction, and a cause. This was the impetus I needed to sustain my efforts and charge my energies for the years to come. I was working — and would continue to work — for decent dignified community living for my child and for all other children who happened to have developmental problems.

There were of course other learnings that took place that summer, and for better or for worse I soaked them all up like a sponge. We were all indoctrinated in the existing knowledge of the day, which put students with mental retardation into compartments for the convenience of school administrators. Schools received average daily attendance moneys based on these classifications, and classes were organized accordingly.

We drew dividing lines hard and fast. Educable mentally retarded children were those with IQs of fifty to seventy. They were considered capable of reading on an elementary level and might become economically and socially independent. Those with the label "trainable" were supposed to have IQs between thirty-five and fifty, and would, we were told, always require a protected environment. Work, marriage, and voting would not be for them. Classes for educable students were often located on a regular school campus. Sometimes we called them opportunity classes. Those for trainable students were placed off by themselves in basements, campers, trailers, or little houses where the students were isolated, protected, and treated like the children they were supposed to be.

We were told that one always correlates chronological age with mental age. Joe Blow, at seventeen years of age, weighing one hundred eighty-five pounds, is still a child if his age places him at the mental age of a five-year old. Nobody told us that an IQ score is just one way of expressing the results of a particular test administered by a particular person and taken by an individual on a particular day. The person administering the test had perhaps never met the child before, and could not factor in any observations about their functioning in school or home environment provided by parents or teacher. The number stuck and determined the fate of the child.

I began to feel uncomfortable about this absolute IQ information for I could tell how it raised and dashed my own hopes for Barbara. I thought then, that as a parent I was too close to my own child to challenge "the professionals" with our own observations of her. As an aspiring special education teacher I came close to being entrapped by the IQ theories of the fifties.

Those in the professional community — special educators and psychologists — had earlier described three broad categories of "mental deficiency" securely tied to IQ scores. It was "idiot" for those scoring below IQ 25, "imbeciles" from 25 to 50, and "morons" from 50 to 70 or 75. By the time I returned to school in 1959, these terms had been shifted from "idiot" to "severe," "imbecile" to "moderate," and "moron" to "mild." We thought we were so progressive in making these changes, and yet we were still putting children and adults into rigid, inflexible boxes, which kept them from any outward and upward movement.

In one respect the new nomenclature was even more restrictive than the old. Not only were people boxed in by the concept, "Once retarded, always retarded," now some of them were further restricted by being classified as, "Once trainable, never educable." Such persons were placed on a narrow, irreversible conveyor belt which dead-ended in repetitive, non-productive learning and precluded hope for further growth. We were actually creating a breeding ground for boredom and inappropriate "behaviors."

It was not until many years later that educators would come to understand many so-called trainable students functioned quite well outside of these IQ cubbyholes in their family homes, neighborhoods, and yes, on their jobs. With that we became aware of a factor above and beyond IQ and the ratio of chronological to mental age. We discovered the importance of "social adaptation," which helped to bring about open-ended programming.

My own eye opener was a slim report that resulted from a high level conference on problems of education of children in the inner city. It was sponsored by the President's Committee on Mental Retardation and the Bureau of Education for the Handicapped. It was held in Virginia in 1969, and the report was called "The Six Hour Retarded Child." It contained gems of conclusions and recommendations that seemed to me to apply to isolated rural areas as much as inner cities:

> We now have what may be called a six-hour retarded child
> — retarded from nine to three, five days a week, solely on the
> basis of an IQ score, without regard to his adaptive behavior,
> which may be exceptionally adaptive to the situation and
> community in which he lives.

Those conference participants were questioning educational practices and ideas which, during that summer session at San Francisco State, I was excitedly swallowing hook, line, and sinker.

- Trainable retarded children have little concept of history or geography. Limit their lessons to the here and now.
- Trainables are less aware of their handicap than educables.
- They have a short attention span.
- Their memory is poor.
- They cannot handle abstractions, draw conclusions, or use judgment.

"Cannot, cannot, cannot," was the refrain — always accompanied by the magical IQ cut-off to strengthen the intellectual compartments into which we were placing these children in our well-intentioned professional wisdom. We unlearned much of this later from our own children and from Barbara's classmates as we taught them and they taught us.

Personally I still respected intelligence tests. To learn to work with them had been part of the requirement for my MA degree in counseling and guidance degree from Teachers College, Columbia University and I had kept the Stanford Binet IQ testing kit. At times I was sorely tempted to use it. It would have been fun to see how bright Karen and David really were, and to double check Barbara's test results. I knew however that such a test — administered by a parent — might be skewed, and so I resisted the temptation.

Both Al and I had been conditioned to believe that smart is better than stupid and that an educated person is worth more than one who is ignorant. Both of our families valued professional education and respected white collar accomplishments. My own brother had had a tough time academically, and it had taken World War II and the G.I. Bill to point him to a successful career in the Foreign Service. Al had never gone to college, had worked hard with his hands most of his life, and was without a doubt the ablest, warmest and most self-reliant man I had ever known.

And yet the IQ myth hung heavily over my head during these early years of Barbara's life. In spite of the fact that I could see her making slow but steady progress, I felt let down if one of her tests scores was a few points lower than the time before. A slight increase raised my hopes. Schools were pressuring families with the expectation that their children with special developmental needs had to qualify for school programs which were rightfully theirs. Barbara was supposed to be ready for school instead of the schools being ready for her.

I had a chance to read one of the psychological reports on Barbara when she was older and being tested to qualify for Social Security benefits. This was a standard one-page assessment prepared by a certified psychologist who saw her only briefly and for the first time. The IQ figure did not come as a surprise, although it had faded into the back of my consciousness over the years of living with my daughter. It was the anecdotal assessment of the report that appalled me. The man who tested Barbara had no way of knowing how she was actually functioning, and how she had grown and changed. He referred to her as "severely retarded" and added a few sentences about the areas in which he considered her "incompetent." The report was totally impersonal, and once more our Barbara disappeared behind a derogatory label.

Barbara celebrates her 23rd birthday

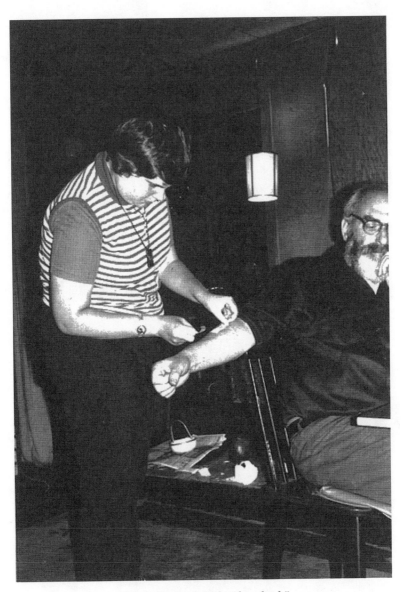

"Helping Dad with a bandaid."

Barbara at 22 with the family

Barbara does ceramics

Chapter 7

Paul Bunyan School

We didn't launch "our" school for another year. The summer at San Francisco State had both encouraged and discouraged me. It had given me lots of theory, but left me short on confidence. The demonstration class which we had observed as students during the summer session seemed so difficult that I thought I could never teach a group like it.

For the summer the special education department had gathered together a group of children from a dozen school districts of San Francisco. They were strangers to each other, and the teacher had no previous experience with them. The children's ages and special needs covered a wide range. Some were very quiet and withdrawn — some uncontrolled. One girl had occasional seizures. There was no teacher's aide. We students sat silently, taking notes, and watched in awe as she pulled this group of children together. I didn't feel ready or able to tackle a comparable task. Some years later I met this teacher again and told her of my trepidation, and how that demonstration had weakened rather than strengthened my own resolve. She laughed and said, "I almost didn't make it myself that summer! I lost twelve pounds in those six weeks!" But neither she nor any of the other faculty members had let on. They did a masterful job of letting us think that this was a breeze, so I came home, realizing I needed allies, and found them.

The first was one of our county's special education teachers, who invited me to visit her class. It was a curvy drive of an hour and a half over the hill and turned out to be well worth it. Mrs. Jamison was not only a great teacher, but an excellent teacher's teacher. She briefly introduced me. "Boys and girls, this is Mrs. Moise from Fort Bragg. She is a teacher too, and is interested in what we are doing." As I headed for the safety of a chair in the corner of the room, she continued, "This is Ruth. She is doing a problem with clocks. Why don't you work with her. Here, take this chair." I was on. She made me a working partner, and it felt comfortably like the practice teaching I had done before. I began to look forward to those weekly trips and after a few months I was able to announce confidently at a parents' meeting, "Let's start our class in the fall."

And then I met my most significant ally — a fellow parent who was to become my staunchest partner for years. We were gathered in our town's Veteran's Memorial Building to be seen by a team of visiting physicians and psychologists from a Northern California State Hospital — again waiting on brown wooden benches. It was a fearfully familiar room to many of the children and they were leery and restless. They had been here before for their baby immunizations and childhood check-ups from the County Public Health doctor. I felt relatively calm, for I expected no new shocks from this visit, but the young mother next to me seemed anxious and apprehensive. We introduced ourselves. Dodie and her husband and son had recently moved to Fort Bragg from out of state. We talked about our children.

"Jeff has a heart murmur," she told me. It's because he's mongoloid (the commonly used term in 1960 for persons with Down Syndrome). Where we lived before the doctor told me he might outgrow it. As a matter of fact, they never said anything to us when Jeff was born. We found out when he had pneumonia at three months and we had to rush him to the hospital. When we asked the doctor how come he hadn't told us earlier, he said he'd just never seen Down Syndrome before. The public health nurse here suggested that I have him evaluated again."

So Dodie and I became friends and partners. She was an experienced primary teacher, while my experience was stronger in working with teenagers and adults. Because she also had a boy who was younger than Jeff, she chose not to work full time yet, but she promised to help me all she could — and she did.

That year I was scheduled to take another step towards my credential — a position as counselor at a summer camp co-sponsored by the San Francisco Association for Retarded Children and the special education department of San Francisco State College. Dodie decided to come too. Tom Murphy and Rita Mattei, two dynamic special education teachers, co-directed the college credit course and camp operation in the hills of Santa Cruz.

We learned a tremendous amount that summer. For many of the students/counselors this was the first time they actually lived with a child or adult with a problem of mental retardation. Here we took care of them "hands on" and around the clock. I found out that disabilities range widely and that there are children whose disability is much more severe than Barbara's. Dodie was a cabin counselor for boys and I worked with girls. We never walked. We ran and huffed and puffed up and down those hills to the bathrooms (this was a scout camp) and I got up extra early some mornings to compete for the sunniest tree branch to dry out wet sleeping bags. I became convinced then that a live-in experience — whether in a camp, group home or with a family — is essential. It should be a mandated prerequisite not only for teachers of persons with developmental disabilities, but also for social workers, psychologists, and agency personnel. It would bridge impasses in gut level understanding, and greatly enhance mutual respect.

At Camp La Honda, in the evening after all the campers were tucked into their cots, those counselors who were working for special education credits gathered in the lodge by the fire to try to tie the day's experiences to the body of theory and methods which Tom and Rita were to impart to us. It didn't work out that way. We'd sit on the floor, huddled in our sweatshirts and doze off. The two wise professors realized that those reading assignments and anecdotal records which they had at first required really weren't all important. What mattered more was for the campers to learn new skills and have a lot of fun under wide-awake supervision. Whether they came from the wards of the state hospital or the shelter of their own homes, here at camp they were expected to do many things they had thought they could not do. Camper and counselor alike experienced growth in shocked surprise. And before one of the camp sessions for young adults was over, I earned the distinction of having a visitor mistake me for a camper, and a camper was taken for a counselor. They couldn't tell us apart in our grubby shorts. Hooray!

I returned to Camp La Honda for a second round of credential credits in 1961. This time I served as recreation counselor, song leader, organizer of fun and games, and booster of enthusiasm. Our children were allowed to come with me. Barbara camped with the little kids for one week, and Karen and David were designated junior, junior counselors for the entire stretch.

Rita, the director, ruled that Barbara's cabin counselor was to make believe I was not there. She wanted Barbara to have the full experience of independence, and she needed me to function efficiently in my work without being distracted by parental worries. This worked out well. I rarely saw or heard from Barbara. She'd give me an off hand wave in the dining room or an embarrassed smile as I hoarsely led the singing at the campfire. Except for one evening.

"Come see Barbara — she's crying," came the SOS. I hurried to her cabin and sat by her. She was already tucked into bed. "What's the matter?" I asked. "I want my prayers!" she wailed. So I launched into our "Now I lay me down to sleep" routine she was used to from home, and she was asleep before I had finished. She too was dead tired after trudging up and down those hills all day and just needed a little reassurance.

The camp turned out to be a mix of work and play for Karen and David. Both of them were messengers deluxe for the directors and staff and trotted many miles. Karen, at twelve, was better able to take direct responsibility for some campers than ten year old David. She could help with dressing and undressing at the swimming pool and in her cabin, and she assisted with arts and crafts. David's major contribution turned out to be his friendship with one of the campers who was a couple of years younger than he. His friend's disability was barely visible in a camp setting. Both David and he liked little cars. David had brought a supply from home, and the two of them pushed cars along dirt race tracks for hours. The two boys' easy summer friendship became an affirmation for us all. Alikeness had indeed transcended their supposed difference.

Both Karen and David glowed with pride when Rita rewarded their efforts with ten dollar salary checks. As a further surprise, the Department of Health, Education and Welfare spun out a Social Security number for David.

Our friends, the Hall family, helped mightily with the coordination of these summer ventures. They had moved to Fresno and their house became a home away from home. Barbara stayed with them after her own camp session was finished, while Karen and David and I worked on. They paid me a visit at La Honda one summer and their eight and nine year old children really liked the camp. "When will we be old enough to be counselors at Barbara's camp?" they wanted to know. They got their chance later when they were teenagers, after the parent associations in our area of Northern California had organized our own camp.

Barbara continued to be a camper for many more summers. She looked forward to it as the high point of her year. She did not get homesick. She did not catch cold. She did not drown. She walked better and spoke more words because she was excited and had more to talk about.

It was at the Halls' home in Fresno that we discovered Barbara was actually able to swim in deep water. When Al and I came to gather up our children, Lloyd Hall asked us to watch Barbara in the pool. "We think she'd be okay in the deep end, but we didn't want to take on the responsibility without you." We went swimming, and the two Dads organized a brisk game of water tag. Four adults and a bunch of kids were chasing each other and the ball in and out around the pool. Big splashes and loud hoops and hollers. "Where's Barbara?" someone asked.

She was calmly floating in the middle of the deep end as if in the eye of a hurricane! Arms tucked around her knees, she was doing a classic Red Cross jellyfish float. I swam up to her anxiously. She was as relaxed as could be. Nice big air bubbles were rising rhythmically around her face, and in between she came up for a breath with a smile. She certainly was ready for the deep end, and everyone congratulated her as if she'd swum the English Channel.

Each year when we arrived at camp, we noticed how quickly she turned away from us to a beloved counselor whom she remembered from a previous year. The reverse happened when we came to get her. Al and I were more excited about the reunion with our little daughter than she seemed to be, as she lingeringly hugged the new friends she had made. She was indeed showing subtle signs of growing into her own life.

When Dodie and I returned to Fort Bragg from our first camp experience in 1960, we were leaner, wiser and determined to open school. I had gained confidence and was not afraid any more. Dodie had met children *and* adolescents who had Down Syndrome and had experienced how much hope there is for their future. I had shared in her joyful surprise during one afternoon quiet period when we were playing restful records for a group of young adults. The music had barely begun when a head came up from the blanket. "That's 'The Sorcerer's Apprentice' by Ducas," announced a so-called retarded camper with authority and lay down again. Dodie and I could hardly believe it.

Dodie did not work at our new school that first year. She wanted to be home with Jeff and his younger brother. So I became the official teacher at three dollars a day (the "board" insisted I should at least have gas money, although our bank account did not contain enough to cover a full year's teaching days), and Dodie became my most valued advisor. We kept the phone busy with daily recaps and planning sessions.

Our school followed the classic pattern of parent-operated ventures. We spoke with an understanding minister, Reverend Kent, who offered us the use of a Sunday School room and a hall closet for storage. We recruited a few willing volunteers and rounded up the students, most of whom were the children of the parent association members and had never been to school. Some had dropped out or been excluded from public school, and others came by word of mouth. We opened our door at the Presbyterian Church in September 1960.

My hands shook a little on that first September morning as I pinned carefully lettered name cards on a cork board and took roll call: "Terry, Penny, Eddie, Russell, Susie, Ernie, Jim, Gary, Helen, Barbara." My ten students sat in a half-circle in front of the board. They were all sizes, shapes, and ages. At six, Barbara was the youngest. Jim towered over her at a lanky eighteen. Some talked a blue streak, while others had few words. They all seemed eager to learn, and I realized it would take a mighty versatile program to fit everyone's need.

"What are you going to call the school?" Karen asked me at home that evening.

"Why call it anything?"

"Mother! You've got to call it something. What if someone asks one of your kids where he goes to school? D'you expect him to say, 'I go to a special class for retarded children in the Presbyterian Church?' "

I had to agree. We needed a name. Karen thought of one from local lumbermen's lore. "Call it the Paul Bunyan School," she suggested.

"Paul Bunyan? Why him? He was huge. Our class is small."

"But Mom — he did the impossible too," she replied. And so it became the Paul Bunyan School.

From the very start Dodie and I decided we would run the school program as well as any public school special class. If the daily minimum attendance requirement for such a class was 180 minutes, we would hold school for three hours. Whatever the education code required we would do — only better. When the public schools became ready to take on responsibility for our children, we'd measure up.

Ten in the morning seemed to be a good time to begin. Most of our parents had more than one child to get off to school. Most of them lived several miles out of town and had to drive their child to our class. I could vouch for the fact that it was certainly a big rush in the mornings. We set the school day for ten until two in the afternoon.

Barbara liked the commotion. While I tore through the house with a dust mop, washed the breakfast dishes, did a little preparatory supper cooking, and figured out a shopping list, she'd stand with her nose glued to the window until Karen's and David's big yellow school bus arrived. Then she'd help me. At six she was unable to put her longing into language, but it was written all over her face that she wished she could go on the bus with them, instead of with me in the old station wagon.

We stayed in that church room from September until the following Easter vacation. We used the room every weekday, and then cleaned and rearranged it for Sunday School use. A few more students joined our ranks, and many, many volunteers. I had to get up a little earlier each Monday morning, because there were so many teaching materials to be set out before the students arrived.

The Friday afternoon stow-away operation into the hall closet became more and more of a challenge. "This week you're not going to make it, Lotte," Mr. Kent would pronounce as he watched me kneeling on the floor surrounded by boxes, rolls of reading charts, piles of construction paper, arithmetic workbooks, crayons, glue, material scraps, and other treasures I had scrounged from the public school supply closets. "Oh ye of little faith," I teased him, and then we'd both push the closet door shut. My own papers, lesson plans, and student records I filed in a grocery carton and carried from school to home and back again.

Barbara blossomed. She, too, could now carry home proof of her progress — finger paintings, lined pieces of newsprint with wobbly letters, and even homework. Karen and David drew her into the suppertime sharing period. "How was school today? What did you do?" One word answers grew into two-word sentences, and speech was on its way. One evening we had invited Father Larsen, the vicar of the Episcopal parish for supper. Dick Larsen loved all young people. He brought along a visiting ministerial friend from out of town, whose one arm was so disabled he could barely use it. "Pass the butter, please," said the friend and proceeded laboriously to pile it on a muffin.

Barbara had been told dozens of times not to use too much butter, so she watched his attempts with great interest. Then — "Too much!" she stated clearly, causing us all laughter, embarrassment and pride.

The Paul Bunyan School students became well known around town that first winter. The church was located on a downtown corner, which lacked any open space for outdoor play and exercise. Both teacher and students desperately needed to get out of that crowded room every day to break the pace and tension of those early experimental weeks. On dry, sunny days we walked five blocks to the slides, swings and basketball hoops of the city playground.

We organized neighborhood field trips. We visited the bakery at doughnut baking time, the train station and the roundhouse, the lumber mill, the firehouse, even the police station and jail. Then we began making a twice weekly soup and sandwich lunch in the church kitchen and shopped for groceries. "Your children are so well behaved. Why, they behave better than my own," we heard. "Look at Jane. She is so much quieter when she comes with the class. You know how she tends to screech when she's with her Mom. See! Gary picked out that can of tomatoes all by himself." The clerks in the store reflected our pride. Thank goodness for a small town. We made up for our makeshift school house with lots of visibility. In fact it was the lack of a fancy facility that gave us valuable contact with the townspeople.

The volunteers who were beginning to assist us took much of my energy and became both a buoying and a draining force. We knew the parents of our students deserved a little rest. We did not yet have any transportation for them, and many of them lived several miles out of town. They told us that by the time they had driven to school it was almost time to turn around and pick their children up again. So we tried to find volunteers who were nonparents. This caused us to do much soul searching. We were beginning to be asked to talk about our program. Social and service clubs, fraternal organizations and study clubs with which Fort Bragg abounded, were always in need of speakers. Dodie and I were often invited and accepted all invitations to tell them about our newfound knowledge. Inevitably someone would ask,

"How come you need so many volunteers? Why can't the parents help more?"

It was a tough one. The lack of transportation was easy enough to explain in the beginning, but it was clearly not the only reason. We continued to need many volunteers long after we had organized a volunteer car pool and had ferreted out an obscure paragraph in the education code which stated that local superintendents "may" provide bus transportation to private schools. Why couldn't or wouldn't we ask more parents to donate their time?

The honest answer was that they were drained. The anxiety and frustration of having a child whose special needs were not being met had taken all the starch out of them and they needed those few school hours to recharge their batteries. When we looked at our roster of families many of them had multiple problems. Several were on welfare. Some simply didn't have the energy and motivation to take part in the overall planning of our association which took place at evening meetings. One of our students with Down Syndrome also had diabetes. His older sister, and the only other child, died of diabetes complications. The death of one man left his widow a single mother — barely able to cope with the care of our student and a hard-to-manage teenage son. One mother began to have a daytime drinking problem, so that I would have to phone and wake her to tell her it was time to come and pick up her daughter. There were two pairs of brothers from two different families enrolled in our class.

Most of our families were poor. Only a small handful of us had the good fortune to be healthy, energetic, affluent, and "together" enough to carry on the Paul Bunyan School project. We were beginning to understand the message being put out by our national organization during the Kennedy administration: *A substantial percentage of so-called "mental retardation" in inner cities is caused by social, cultural or economic deprivation.* This applies to isolated rural areas also, and to this day the problem has not been solved.

We continued to recruit volunteers. Their schedules had to be precise and tight. Although helpers could give as little or as much time as they chose, I insisted they phone me ahead if they were unable to make it so I could line up a substitute. I encouraged them to ask me questions and assured them it did not necessarily take a college degree to teach our students the practical skills which they themselves possessed. I spent much time on the phone in the afternoon when I returned home from school, and we developed a fine team of volunteers — simply trained but loyal and full of energy.

I had to learn the hard way that there were certain drawbacks to relying on volunteers. You couldn't fire them. So we tried to develop criteria for choosing from among the townspeople who were interested and had answered our invitation to "come see what we are doing — and help."

It all started with the swimming program. I had a hunch, based on my experience as a Red Cross water safety instructor, that our students would be able to learn to swim. It was an activity with which I had overcome my own poor coordination. I thoroughly believed in its therapeutic effect, and besides we agreed that some of our students needed showers. The municipal pool was funky, but it was indoors and heated. I was pleased at the Recreation Department's lack of opposition. "As long as you have your Red Cross water safety certificate and have plenty of volunteers, why not?" I assured them we planned to have one adult with each child, and they promised to cover us with their insurance.

We decided to stage a "dry run" for our students in preparation for the great first swim day. We'd walk to the pool and show our youngsters the dressing rooms and showers and they could watch a coach teach a class. Two middle-aged matrons happened to be the scheduled volunteers for that day. "Swimming!" they exclaimed in unison. "Don't you think that's too dangerous?" I could have cheerfully muzzled them both since several of our students were within earshot, but I confined myself to a mutter and tried to maneuver them into a corner. There we continued our conversation.

The problem was both women were so full of good intentions. They had been among the first to step forward when we needed help, and they were dependable and punctual. What's more, they were power figures in our small town. Their husbands were prominent

71

businessmen who belonged to the service club that had promised to hold a major fund-raising event on our behalf. How do you tell such a volunteer that she should think before she speaks? Their outspoken personal doubts and apprehensions piled on top of our students' self-doubts were devastating to them. So we learned to prepare for swim days, which happened to be "their" day, by having plenty of other helpers on board to run interference. From then on I screened volunteers.

I asked each potential new helper to spend a few hours of a school day with us before we put them on the schedule. We observed their reactions and those of our students towards them. Then we'd sit down and talk. "Those poor children!" smacked of pity, and we didn't want our children to be pitied. We looked for cheerful, practical, positive people who could instinctively recognize our students' potential for growth. They outnumbered the others by far. And I learned to side-track those with negative reactions into helping us in ways which did not involve much participation in one-on-one teaching activities. "Oh, thank you. I'm so glad you came. We desperately need help in our thrift shop. And we could use a cake and some cookies for our next holiday party, as well as assistance at our fundraising events."

Someone asked me one day, "What makes a good volunteer for your program, Lotte?" By then we had added high school helpers to our recreation and swim programs. I noticed many of them seemed to come from the troubled and troublesome fringe of the school population: the kind of kids who nowadays might elect to go to alternative school. "I think it has to do with understanding hurt," I said. "Yes, our best volunteers have experienced trouble and know about feeling devalued."

All this seems like ancient history to me now. Some of our first students have grown into adults who actually take part in the process of planning for the programs that support them. In California our entitlement legislation, the Lanterman Act, has been revised to mandate their membership on boards and councils. Self Advocates all over the country and in many countries of the world, have become empowered to sit at the table with those who make the decisions — even on per-

sonnel interview committees for staff persons whom *they* help to select. They have gone on record as saying they want to be advised —
not controlled.

Susan was an exceptional volunteer. She shone at home, on the
school campus, and as a volunteer at our school. She had been one of
the neighbor children in our nursery school car pool, and she and Barbara had remained friends. So when she decided to do a science report
on "mental retardation" when she was in junior high school, she came
to see me to ask about some of the particulars of our school curriculum and inadvertently taught me a big lesson and radically changed
my thinking.

"How come your school is off by itself?" she wanted to know. By
then we had moved out of the church and into our own building — a
small frame bungalow on a residential side street — just a few blocks
from her school.

I gave Susan my best special education teacher answer, gleaned
from my studies and the prevailing theory of the day: "Shelter, protection from hurt, homelike environment."

She wrote it all down and then looked up: "Do you think Barbara
could carry a tray in a cafeteria line?" she asked.

"Yes, now she could. I don't think she could have done it a few
years ago, but I saw her do it when we ate in a cafeteria in the city not
long ago, and she did okay." The question puzzled me. "Why do you
ask?"

Her answer came slowly and thoughtfully. "Well then, why
couldn't she go to our school? It seems to me you're protecting us from
something we shouldn't be protected from. You don't protect us from
crippled children or deaf or blind children. Why do you protect us
from retarded children?"

From the mouth of a twelve-year-old I heard the first mention of
"mainstreaming." If only we had heard her insight sooner.

The real learning for us all began when we moved from the church
room to a real house of our own. Now we had a living-dining room
combination, two small bedrooms, a kitchen, a backyard, and a
woodshed. We also had fifteen students and volunteers with varied

talents, whom I remember with pleasure and gratitude. We did some fancy grouping to accomplish individualized programs and used every inch of space in that small house. We even moved a cot into the bathtub so it could double for rest or "time out," provided it wasn't being used for tooth brushing practice or other bathroom activities. From the group of regular volunteers, we chose four women whom we employed to teach full time for one week of each month. They prepared careful lesson plans and rotated. Dodie's husband and some of the older boys built a wooden deck in the lumpy backyard so we'd have a level space to dance and exercise in good weather. Various community organizations brought us play equipment. We planted a garden. We cooked lunch every day now, and the woodshed became a working woodshop.

The wide ability and age range of our fifteen students put a tremendous load on our program and at the same time kept us from getting into a rut. Our volunteer faculty were able to recognize the students' changing program needs and contributed their own skills and resources to our curriculum. "Helen embroiders so well, couldn't we teach her to hem and sew up pillow cases? My sister-in-law has this old treadle machine she says she'd let us use." And we gained a sewing machine and a new activity for Helen. "Eddie is real handy with a splitting ax and a hatchet, and this place is pretty chilly every morning. Why don't we make him responsible for bringing in the kindling for the fireplace and the woodstove from the shed? His mom says he takes care of that at home." And soon Eddie was not only preparing the wood, but also getting the fire going in the morning.

We were actually beginning to organize several programs under one roof. In the front bedroom I taught beginning academic skills to students who seemed able to handle reading and numbers. Our four rotating teachers taught the other crew in the back bedroom. This included Barbara and worked out well so she wasn't always being taught by her own mother. Actually, the matter of teaching my own child did not bother me too much, having been trained in the British tradition of home teaching. Together all of our students took part in the morning opening program of warm-up exercises, discussion of the weather, the calendar numbers and days, and "show and tell," of course. Anything that encouraged speech and participation. We then planned the most important activity of the day — lunch preparation.

In the afternoon the older students branched out into a more vocationally oriented track. By then we knew the top permissible age for a public school class would be twenty-one. Several of our young men and women were either pushing that age or were already in their early twenties. One or two of them were showing signs of restlessness at going to school with a bunch of little kids. Academic skills bored them, but they did well at practical chores.

A primitive vocational program evolved naturally. Our parent association's fundraising thrift shop provided an opportunity for sorting donated clothes, washing them in the laundromat, and then ironing. We heard from a friendly nursery man that leaf mold would sell well to the many commercial fuchsia and rhododendron nurseries on the coast, and this became a project for our young men. Leaf mold results from many layers of redwood needles, which, when left over the years, become a thick springy turf and fine protective mulch for plants. We borrowed a pickup truck, acquired pitchforks and spades, begged for old gunny sacks from the feed store, and went out to harvest and sell the stuff.

A neighbor who had been disabled in a woods accident and was in a wheelchair, became one of our most valued teachers. He heard of our school and volunteered to teach carpentry to the older boys. Since he himself had overcome radical changes in his own life and had never babied himself, he wasn't about to pity or overprotect our young men. Twice a week they walked several blocks unescorted to his shop to learn from him. A respected, retired restaurant owner became the teacher for the thrift shop training program.

Fundraising and scrounging supplies became a bore, as we drooled over catalogues of fancy equipment which we coveted but could not afford. There were times when we were inundated with donations we couldn't use. The towns' people were somehow locked into thinking all "retarded" children like to make scrapbooks out of old greeting cards. "I've been saving my Christmas cards for many years and thought you could use them." Of course we accepted with thanks. Wallpaper books were another favorite and did come in handy, but we had our own storage problems. We'd get an urgent call from a store. "Our new wallpaper sample books just came in. If you come right now you can have the old ones, but you'd better hurry 'cause we've gotta get rid of the old ones." With that we'd dispatch someone to pick them up, even if it meant a stealthy trip to the dump at dusk to dispose of unwanted items.

Our small school even came to the attention of the producer of *The Russians Are Coming! The Russians Are Coming!* when it was being filmed in Mendocino and Fort Bragg. They had a problem with the box lunches for their many extras. On the days when the fog rolled in over the coast, they needed to send many of them home for the day. What to do with the lunches? I was ready to close school one day when a truck pulled up and delivered a small mountain of pink cardboard cartons. Each contained a couple of sandwiches, some fruit, a cupcake, and a candy bar. The school's refrigerator was a home-sized hand-me-down. I SOSed a couple of friends for help. They came and we sorted, bagged, and then borrowed freezer space. There were many more foggy days and deliveries of pink box lunches. We were still eating movie cupcakes well over a year later.

Our program grew rounder and richer when Dodie recruited a friend as a second "curriculum consultant." She too was a primary teacher, busily raising a small family before she returned to work. They taught me the fine art of making large experience charts for reading lessons. It became part of our morning opening session to record the students' own shared happenings of their daily lives, and then use it as a reading lesson. I even found I could illustrate them with stick figures that helped to tell the stories. Together we discovered the value of singing and music for speech development. Tape recorders were like magic mirrors as they played back, "My name is Dan (or John, or Helen). I live in Fort Bragg." over and over, clearer and clearer.

When it was too rainy to use the deck outside, we exercised indoors. I found a record with peppy music and instructions for calisthenics which could be done while standing between the desks. I set such an enthusiastic example with the arm-fling exercise that next spring my dresses were too tight across my ample chest, though I had lost a few pounds. From then on I faked that exercise!

Soon we realized the ancient Greeks' theory "a sound mind in a sound body" also worked for our students, so along with swimming and calisthenics, dancing became a high point of the week. From simple round and square dances to waltzes and rock, we tried them all. Don Frye became our smooth and elegant volunteer teacher. Jane was his most talented and graceful partner for the waltz. Norma and Barbara preferred the rhythm of drum beats. A couple of the guys were reluctant to join in at first, but soon loosened up. Friday afternoons we piled up the desks and chairs and danced. Then we all went home relaxed and smiling.

With the help of my two academic "consultants" we also stumbled onto a form of assessment and evaluation of our students' work. Again it was Karen and David who tipped us off to the need for what we now refer to as "outcomes." "Are you going to give your kids report cards?" they wanted to know. By then some of our students were riding public school buses and Karen and David thought it would be terrible for Barbara and her schoolmates to go home empty-handed on report card day.

Little did they realize what they had started. The reporting process was time consuming and hard work. We searched our souls as we began to clarify our aims and objectives for our students. We threw out letter grades in favor of statements of skills, broadly grouped in the areas of social skills, physical and emotional health, work habits, recreational activities, and skills for economic self-sufficiency.

Under social skills we might comment on Jane's poise and charming manner of greeting visitors. Terry received credit for new words and sentences. Table manners, grooming and speech were given specific, detailed comments.

Under the heading of physical and emotional health, we paid attention to coordination and reported to parents on improvements in specific exercises and dances. Everybody had to brush his or her teeth after lunch. One girl had screamed and fussed at the mere sight of a toothbrush. I had to take her in a vise grip and do it for her. She was now able to do it herself — gingerly. Fingernails looked cleaner and shorter, and we said so on the report card.

The section on work habits included comments on promptness, cleanliness, getting along with others, and following directions. "Following Directions" became a favorite game. "Take this pencil, John, and give it to Mrs. Moise. Then open the front door. Come back inside and bring a book to Mrs. Cain." The report card would state, "John can now follow three directions in a row."

Under recreational activities we listed accomplishment in crafts (cutting with scissors, pasting neatly, coloring within lines, finger painting and clay sculpting), swimming, bowling, and simple table games, which took the place of outdoor games on many rainy afternoons. Actually there was little need to comment on bowling, since their score sheets — carried home triumphantly — gave ample proof of phenomenal progress. Jeff and several other little ones began their bowling careers by placing the ball between their crouched legs and pushing it down the alley. Before long they were standing and swinging the ball and proudly pointing to spares and strikes on the score sheet. In time many of them garnered trophies (Norma called them "sophies") at state Special Olympics tournaments, and far outbowled me. Swimming reports were equally impressive. We recruited many volunteers from the ministerial association and from the police department (who were able to give us time during the day), and with their patience and encouragement most of our students eventually became deep water swimmers.

There was a long list of items under the heading of skills for economic self-sufficiency. Terry learned to tell time by the half and quarter hour. Ernie and Richard were learning to read real books. Barbara could recognize "stop" and "go." Gary was able to distinguish "men" from "women." Jim could endorse a check with a legible signature. Everyone was improving in the many tasks having to do with cleanup, cooking, gardening, and wood work. We tried to teach even the young ones to "tie up the bundle" (do a job from beginning to end).

Rather than handing them the broom, we asked them to please fetch it, do the job, and put it away. Time and time again we reminded ourselves and each other we intended to relate all learning to the children's future needs.

We had objectives for the parents too, and sometimes they were harder work to achieve. For years they had held low expectations and frustration in their hearts. It was hard to change and to realize that they could and should become active partners in the school. We composed a list of objectives for parents:

- To accept the child the way he or she is.
- To accept the child's limitations and not to push the child beyond them.
- To see the child's positive qualities and talents and to make the most of them.
- To interpret our program to other homes and the whole community.
- To face the future.

All of this took hours, but it was worth it. We invited the parents to come to school for individual conferences, during which we talked with them about their son's or daughter's strong or weak spots and urged them to support our school program with home practice. Then we folded the reports into small manila envelopes scrounged straight from the public school supply closet, and the students carried them home "just like the other kids."

Sewing a button

Barbara dictates a letter. I print it. She copies it.
Hard work, but she has things to say

Chapter 8

Balloons and Bubbles

We sent up many balloons and experienced lots of burst bubbles during the first four years of the Paul Bunyan School. Our students burst most of the bubbles, but all of us — students, teachers, volunteers, parents, and towns-people — contributed concepts and ideas bright as balloons.

I graduated from my cardboard grocery carton to a donated green file cabinet that locked. In it we kept confidential files on each of our students. They contained report cards, information on test scores, medical information, parent release forms for publicity photos, and permission slips for field trips, swimming, and the use of potentially dangerous tools such as power lawn mowers and saws.

The more I came to know our students, the more their IQ scores faded into the background. New helpers and visitors would inevitably ask about them, and often I blanked. I was not getting forgetful or trying to make a point. Those numbers were simply becoming non-vital statistics in my thinking. The planning that made the complex school program function — who could perform certain tasks, how we might recruit another helper to teach a needed skill — was uppermost in my mind. Inevitably we saw our students as individuals — as persons. Today "person-centered-planning" has become a buzz word, but we were doing it then.

We had no choice. Several of our students were big active country boys with little interest in book learning, but they understood the significance of work and money. The sooner we could move them toward earning a living the better. Jim, for example, hated to sit still. Contrary to what we had been told in college — "trainable students are less aware of their deficits than those who are educable" — he seemed extremely sensitive about his previous school failures. And yet he was an anchor man when it came to doing chores and giving practical advice. On our very first field trip I realized I'd be much better off lost in the woods with Jim than with most of my friends. He was dependable, resourceful, and responsible for our younger students. Even during those days of the early sixties Dodie and I expressed our hunch that his so-called mental retardation and that of several of our other students resulted from their impoverished background, total lack of cultural stimulation at home, and poor health care and nutrition.

For Easter that first spring we received one of our questionably useful gift from a pet store owner. He came to school in person, bearing a cardboard box. We welcomed drop-in visitors; they were a bit distracting but helped spread the word about our program. So I barely glanced inside the carton and thanked him for the donation. Later I discovered the box was filled with moving multicolored fluff. The well meaning merchant had given us a half dozen chicks dyed for Easter.

They soon outgrew their colored down and turned into plain white hens — noisy, hungry, thirsty, smelly, and dirty. Again we "scrounged" and placed a hand-me-down chicken coop in the far corner of the backyard. Jim became their keeper. He did a great job. Responsible as usual, he'd have the dirty trays emptied and filled with feed and water before I even came to school early in the morning. One day I complimented him. "You're doing such a good job, Jim. I've been thinking I might talk to one of our neighbors about you. He has a chicken ranch. I may be able to get you a job there." Jim looked glum and shook his head. "Don't you like to work with chickens?"

He continued shaking his head. "Nah, Moise, I *hate* chickens. I wanna work with cars!"

There went the first bubble. Who was planning for whom? I was obviously caught up in the same stereotyped thinking as the rest of the world. "Let's let blind people weave baskets!" What right did I have to plan for Jim's future without considering his own interests? We gave away those chickens, and Jim eventually went to work for a body and fender business.

We had planned our school day for four hours because the attention span of "trainables" was not supposed to extend beyond that. Within a short time we found that far too short. To squeeze in all our varied activities we stretched the school day to six hours. Of course, the students stretched right along with the schedule.

The reading program turned out to be another surprise. I had been taught to teach only survival words such as stop and go, hot and cold, men and women and so forth, but both Richard and Ernie were clearly interested in stories. They moved rapidly from flash cards with single words through primers to real books. I was pretty excited by this unexpected breakthrough and began to push them on. One day I told Ernie to hurry up with his reading. He looked up from his book accusingly. "I'm doing my best, Moise!" The student was telling the teacher to ease the pressure. From then on we scheduled time for reading "just for fun." We read aloud story books to them and read and talked about interesting items from the weekly local newspaper. Ernie clearly liked Peter Pan best of all and that is how I learned another lesson.

He came to school one morning with a big bruise on the side of his face. "What happened?" we all asked.

"Well, I wanted to try again," he said.

"Try what, Ernie?"

"Fly like Peter Pan. I climbed a tree. I wanted to fly down like him." Pop goes another bubble. Who was it that claimed "retarded" youngsters have no imagination?

The same expert, I think, came up with the theory of limiting teaching to the here and now. "Nothing beyond the immediate neighborhood will have meaning for your students." That went out the window the summer Barbara went to summer camp while I accompanied my mother on a trip to Hawaii. As Al and the children were seeing us off, Barbara piped up, "Bring me a funapple, Mom!"

"A what-did-you-say?"

"A funapple," she repeated emphatically, making a circular motion with her hands. "She means a pineapple," David interpreted. "She knows they have 'em there."

After we were all home again, I heard a yell from the living room where Barbara was watching TV. "Mom! Come! Hawaii on TV!" And sure enough there'd be a hula girl under a palm tree or a surfer. Barbara clearly connected them with Hawaii — hardly her immediate neighborhood.

We then began to reach beyond our neighborhood with plans for field trips. By then we had established an advisory board of community business men to help us with fundraising and other financial matters. At first they shook their heads in doubt and disapproval when we suggested a trip to the zoo in San Francisco. "Next you'll be wanting to take them to Disneyland," they clucked. Dodie and I bit our lips and touched knees under the table. That is exactly where we wanted to go — to Disneyland and the planetarium, to snow country, out on a boat and up in a plane. "Here and now" was for the birds!

It was Dodie and her family who proved us right. Her husband switched careers from teaching to commercial fishing and sailing. He built a sailboat and when Jeff and his younger brother were teenagers, the family spent an entire year sailing all over the Pacific. Jeff charmed all the girls on the islands where they docked. Travel with his folks became the high point of his life.

All along we provided a great deal more for our students than a stimulating learning environment. We tried to bolster their self esteem in many ways to let them know they were valued. Every one of them had a birthday party at school with a cake and candles and a carefully thought out present. Santa Claus came at Christmas time and brought each person a gift. We became so caught up in doing for them that we almost forgot something important: it is demeaning to be always on the receiving end. "Allbody" (a word Barbara coined) enjoys the joy of giving. A friend told me this story. She had once taken an institutionalized young woman who had a disability for an outing to a tea shop. There was a wishing well in the garden and she offered her young friend a coin to throw in. "Now you have to make a wish," she said, and then, "What did you wish for?"

And this was what the girl said: "I wish I could treat someone to a soda some day!"

Among our students it was Richard who first expressed his wish to do for others. Our school district provided a home teacher for five youngsters with physical disabilities. Their teacher approached me to ask if they might use the backyard of the Paul Bunyan School for their annual party. Her boys wanted to have a wheelchair softball game, with their mothers running the bases as the boys batted from their chairs. "Why couldn't *we* do it, Mrs. Moise? Why couldn't we do the running for them?" Richard wanted to know. And so it happened — a fine two-inning ballgame, a picnic and a few songs to wind up the afternoon. Richard had a big smile on his face which clearly expressed his joy at being on the giving end for a change.

Later, another of our young men made this point even more forcefully. Bob was a moody young man with a temper. On one of those days when nothing went right for him, I heard the work supervisor reprimand him and Bob blew his stack. I walked outside with him to help him cool off. We stood on the steps and talked about the situation. Nothing seemed to penetrate his sulking. "Hey, Bob," I said. "Mr. Bunner (his woodshop teacher) tells me he has almost finished straightening the spokes on your bike wheel. You should have it back by tomorrow." I knew Bob's bike was his prize possession and thought this news would help.

"I don't care!" he burst out, "And I'm sick and tired of being helped!"

The teachers of the Paul Bunyan School learned many more concepts from each other and from our students. We learned they had the right to move on and up. Richard was the first to be admitted into a public school special class and we missed him terribly. He was so articulate and bright and cheerful. How would we ever do the morning "share and tell" period without him? To add insult to injury he now avoided speaking to me when we met downtown. He was so proud of going to regular school that his former association with us embarrassed him.

Richard has come a long way. At first I'd see him at the downtown library checking out an armful of books. He became manager of the high school football team. Then he moved to a neighboring town where he now lives in his own apartment, has a job, and manages his own affairs with counseling support as the need arises. His parents have moved to Hawaii and he flies to visit them. Last year, when I received a Woman-of-the-Year award, it was Richard who said he was proud of me! He brought flowers for the occasion and wrote me a card. Certainly it was our letting go that had freed him to grow.

Not all of our students moved away from us so early. Some graduated to the work activity center which was run by our Parent Association once the Paul Bunyan School became part of the school district. We experienced surprises there too. One young man kept arriving at the center earlier than anyone else. He'd wait for a staff person to open the place, and one morning he said, "If you let me have a key, I could open up and have the place all warm by the time we get started." Consternation! It seemed unusual, almost inappropriate for a "client" to assume a "staff" responsibility. We thought about it and then gave him this small but significant assignment.

Another young man asked if he could attend our weekly staff meetings. "I'm really interested in a lot of that stuff — and our money troubles." Surprise again! It had truly become "our" center. He felt part of it, and if we were honestly expecting him to manage on his own in the community perhaps it wouldn't hurt to expose him to our funding worries and other concerns. Both these young men began to attend staff meetings, and gradually certain staff/client differences eroded to the benefit of us all. We tried to solve our problems jointly as co-workers. One of them now occasionally gives me a breezy wave from his pickup truck as we pass on the street. The other is married and touches base more often in a neighborly, friendly way. He still has problems, but I have remained part of his local support system.

It took many small happenings to strengthen my belief in community living. One afternoon, when Barbara was still small, I stopped to say "hi" to a person I knew from my PTA activities. Kathleen has a large birthmark covering her mouth and chin, and I had always admired her poise and presence at social gatherings. Barbara had never met her and I could read the question marks in her eyes. But Kathleen was a jump ahead of me. "Let Barbara ask, Lotte," she said, as she noticed my restraining hand on my child's arm." It looks strange and different to her." And to Barbara she patiently explained the nature of her birthmark and why it couldn't be fixed. She even encouraged Barbara to touch her face.

It dawned on me that day that if Kathleen could run the gauntlet of thoughtless stares and tactless comments, perhaps Barbara and her peers would learn to do the same, but that it would take a lot of public education and awareness building. It still requires stubborn, steadfast advocacy on the part of all of us to convince legislators and administrators that "our sons and daughters are more *like* others than they are different."

I have become increasingly sure over the years that we will not be able to shield our children from real life. If we want them to live outside of institutions in their home communities, they will run the risk of being teased, and of having their feelings hurt.

At that point I was beginning to tumble onto the concept of "risk taking," which Robert Perske later found to be the cornerstone of Scandinavian community programs.

We did not learn all our lessons from our own children and our students. At times we reached out for expert advice from "old pros" in the field of mental retardation. Dodie and I began to look ahead and worry about our students' adult years way back in 1963. Where and how would they live when their parents were gone? Perhaps we could persuade someone to donate land and then get some wealthy angel to erect a few buildings. Could we start a farm operation and combine it with a home for adults? We directed our questions to the source of all wisdom, Professor Gunnar Dybwad, who was at the time the executive director of the National Association for Retarded Children (now the *Arc of the U.S.*).

He and his wife Rosemary — both giants in their field — became mentors and friends to thousands of parents world wide. They worked with an international health organization in Switzerland as advisors. They returned home to teach at the Heller School for Human Development at Brandeis University. Gunnar twinkles when he lectures and pounds the lectern when he testifies. He has been a vehement spokesman at congressional hearings and class action law suits, as he supports and affirms citizen rights of people with disabilities. His wife Rosemary, gracious and quiet, became his research and resource assistant and was largely responsible for the creation of The International League of Societies for the Mentally Handicapped. Now in his eighties, Gunnar is still a lifeline to me at the other end of the telephone in Boston. I miss his wife, Rosemary, who died a few years ago, more than I can say.

So, in 1963, it was to Professor Dybwad that we wrote for advice about our young students' future, and he fired back the following reply:

> Lifetime security cannot be bought for any mortal being, be he sick or well, brilliant or retarded. We can attempt to provide, and his parents have a responsibility to do so, but I want to speak very frankly. It seems to me that in some of your planning there seems to be implied a greater desire for 'peace of mind' on your part as parents than a genuine understanding of what a retarded person should be assured first of all — an opportunity to achieve his fullest potential in life.
>
> The needs of mentally retarded individuals differ sharply. The fact that twelve children age eight to 16 years are now in a privately sponsored class by no means allows us to predict that 20, 15 or even ten years from now these twelve children have the same needs which can be or should be accomplished in the same setting. For some of them, undoubtedly, the facility you picture (*whatever* your picture may be) maybe just the right thing, but for others both the location and the type of facility will prove to be an unnecessary restriction on their God given right to lead as full a life as they are capable of living...
>
> Let me make myself clear. It might be quite possible for your group to start a residential facility as long as the various members of your group are not entertaining the fallacious

idea that by so doing they can count on a permanent haven for their particular child.

We heard Dr. Dybwad's message and dropped the idea of creating a premature "haven." But in other parts of the world the idea of special communities has taken hold in attempts to provide permanence and lifetime security for both parents and their sons or daughters.

Jean Vanier, a deeply religious and spiritual Canadian, began the *L'Arche* communities in France in 1964. They are an international federation of communities where people with learning disabilities and those who choose to spend their lives with them, live and work together. There currently exist 104 *L'Arche* communities in 26 countries worldwide. The men and women Vanier recognizes as "the wounded ones" live in harmony with their "assistants" some of whom make *L'Arche* a commitment for life.

I have visited *L'Arche* homes in London, Toronto and Tacoma, Washington. I know a widowed mother in Australia who worked tirelessly for "public" community programs for her son and has now opted for a *L'Arche* home for him. In Belfast I visited a Rudolf Steiner farm community very like the one Dodie and I envisioned when we wrote to Gunnar Dybwad. They too have established themselves as an alternative to large residential "facilities" and precarious community homes in a sincere effort to meet parents' yearning for permanence for their sons and daughters.

In the meantime we had our hands full with our daily school work, and it wasn't always smooth sailing. We had to make hard choices when our skills and resources proved to be inadequate.

One of our early students was a girl who had frequent and uncontrolled seizures. The other children took these in stride better than we did, but in addition to the seizures she often acted like a whirling dervish of hyper-activity. Because we had minimal access to either medical or psychological consultation services we sadly decided that we could not handle her in our program. It was too risky. We hated the feeling of admitting our failure, but we sent her home again.

The relationship with the parents of our students wasn't always smooth either. I had to juggle my two hats of parent and teacher. On the parent level I understood. Under my teacher hat I sometimes carried my new-found torch of "professional" knowledge too far and pushed too hard. We knew that Ann could eat with a fork, brush her own teeth, and put on her clothes. She did some of these things at school, but her mother would not or could not help her practice these skills at home. We bootlegged the services of the county school psychologist for one afternoon, so that he might counsel both of Ann's parents. They came, but it seemed his advice ran like water off a duck's back. Ann has grown into a tall, good looking young woman. She has come a long way, but the partnership between school and home should have been stronger for her sake.

John's mother was another difficult person. I pushed her hard, perhaps too hard, to work with her son. She never cooperated with us, and after a couple of years I learned to accept reality. She was as tough as a brick wall, hostile, and not to be fooled with. All her life had been rough and uphill, and I am sure that she viewed my snug little family and "professional" motherhood as a threat. I became the target of her irrational outbursts, and she placed John back in a state institution.

One boy's father ran us off his land with a shotgun! Dodie and I had driven out to try one more time to get the old man's permission for his son to have his adenoids and tonsils removed. Joe — according to the Public Health Service physician — already had a fifty percent hearing loss in one ear, and the other was failing too. He had an astigmatism which should have been corrected long ago, but his father stubbornly refused to give permission for these procedures. "Just think of what this will do for your boy's future," we pleaded. "It may make the difference between his being able to stand on his own two feet, or being dependent for life." The shotgun was our answer, and Joe did not have the surgery.

In 1964 we reached a turning point. The County Superintendent of Schools informed us that there was now sufficient funding to make us a county public school. They would paint the Corry Street house inside and out. We'd get a new linoleum floor, much needed equipment and a standard salary for the teacher and her aides. After four years of skimping on our own — after all the hat sales, cake sales and rummage sales we should have been overjoyed, but we were not and we came close to turning him down. We really had become attached to our free wheeling curriculum, impromptu outings, and general freedom. So we hesitated.

It took a wise fellow parent and co-worker, Ray Hudson from the county seat, to persuade us to go under the county schools' umbrella. In Ukiah, he said, great harmony prevailed between parents and schools. Perhaps our program was a little more varied, a bit more creative, he conceded, but how long would we be able to sustain the tremendous effort of our fundraising requirements that drained our energies. He reminded us that some of our students had reached California's maximum school age. Would they now have to be excluded from the program and go home to sit around as they had done before? "Over our dead bodies!" we said, and opted for the security of the county schools' umbrella. And why not let the public schools assume the responsibility that they rightfully should, and that we firmly believed in? Then came the clincher! If our association handed over the operation of the Paul Bunyan School to the county, we would be free to take the next step — a work training program for those of our adults who had outgrown school and were ready for a program appropriate to their age.

So, gradually and incrementally our students have become public school students. It obviously did not happen overnight. The school continued in the same little house for a while — then on to a trailer on a school site. Students with developmental needs now go to school on a Fort Bragg school district campus where they are as "mainstreamed" as individually possible. Full "inclusion" with their peers is still a bone of contention in many places across the land. It still requires strenuous advocacy on the part of parents. The law of the land, however, now stands behind parents, students, and progressive school administrators. Barbara would have loved being "included" as are the many of the students of today.

The work activity center which we launched in the mid-sixties is now incorporated as Parents and Friends, Inc. or Cypress Street Center. It is a multi-faceted program of vocational, residential and living skills activities, attended by young men and women from up and down the Mendocino Coast area. It is accredited by the California Department of Rehabilitation and "vendorized" (which dreadful word means funded) by one of California's twenty-one Regional Centers. It still requires the strenuous support of its local board of directors. They still carry the responsibility of raising funds over and above the support of the State in order to provide quality to the lives of our citizens with special needs, and a modicum of security to the staff persons who believe in their potential for growth. Many balloons, many bubbles later, we have taken a big step towards the dream of the good life for our sons and daughters in their hometowns. Some have ventured to the county seat 55 miles away where they have jobs and live in group homes or apartments. One or two serve as members of the board of directors of the agency that provides their services and support. They have a vote and a voice.

Homework with Al

Proud Papa

Special Olympics, 1980

Chapter 9

The Six Rs

Meanwhile life continued at our house on Sherwood Road. I think back now and wonder how I ever mustered the energy to do justice to both the school house and the home house. Even shopping lists became confusing. "Is this peanut butter supposed to be for our house or for the school?" I was forever asking Barbara if it was okay to borrow one of her toys or books or puzzles or phonograph records to take to school until I realized that I was violating her right of possession. Christmas came and she was pulling her new red wagon around the house when she turned to me and asked. "Keep this home, Mom?" I got the message.

Without Al's and the children's cooperation and the support of our baby-sitters and friends, we might not have hung together as a family. We all knew of marriages that had split up under the stress of a disabled child. We heard about children who felt overwhelmed and embarrassed by a disabled sibling who seemed to deprive them of their parents' love and attention. I would be lying if I gave the impression that Al and I never argued or that our children did not cause us pain. But we survived, and now I can see how we learned, what we learned, and from whom.

I wish I could confidently say that our generation's pioneering advocacy efforts have eliminated all pain and confusion for the young parents of today. Not so. I bristle when I hear it said that the "young parents of today" are not sufficiently motivated and involved. That they don't appreciate the services and supports that exist for them. To-day I go to a meeting of a small local group of mothers who call them-selves PEP, "Parents Empowering Parents." They are legally incorporated under that name as a non-profit, tax-free organization. Some of them are single mothers who hold down jobs too. Their chil-dren's disabilities seem more difficult by far than were my child's at that age.

Research into specific disabilities has become more fine-tuned than it was when Barbara was small. Her problem was labeled "moderate mental retardation — etiology unknown." The young mother who leads the PEP group has a child with a condition called "Angelman's Syndrome" that even some neurologists have only recently become aware of, and of which only about a hundred cases have been identi-fied nationwide. It's a tough one. Her beautiful little girl is non-verbal, very, very quick and active and needs constant supervision — and — she sleeps only about four hours in a twenty-four hour day. For me that might have led to the ultimate defeat of placing my child out of our home. I'll never know, but I am convinced that this is a gutsy Mom and that life is *not* conspicuously easier for her than mine was. The complexity and confusion of the service system that has grown from our pioneering efforts of thirty years ago weighs as heavily on some of the PEP Moms as did the void of services that we had to face.

In our family it became a five-way learning process. Barbara taught us to observe and listen. Like a Jack-in-the-box, she popped out of her "trainable" cubbyhole and blew my neat professional preconceptions to the four winds. Now that these constraints are gone, I can recog-nize the six Rs which helped our house become a home: right to re-spect, regard for differences of opinion, room for differences, risk taking, responsibility, and readiness for role changes.

First there was the *right to respect*. Respect means to "value" and to be worthy of esteem. Between mates in marriage it is considered a foregone conclusion. Respect can grow, even when passion and ro-mantic love have cooled. But when is it time to respect our children? Is it ever too early to see them as persons?

Once I came into David's room and found him sitting on his bed, doing nothing at all, after I had told him to change his clothes "right now!" When I burst out angrily at his dawdling, he looked at me earnestly and said, "Mom, I need to have some time to think."

Karen, an A student, doggedly tried to work on her own coordination. Starting with her tiny tricycle, then stilts, later a bike, tumbling, diving, and mastering her big, stubborn horse, she irritated us to the point of anger with her persistence. It took us years to realize that she was trying so hard because she was hell-bent to overcome what she experienced as her own handicap.

Barbara's low-gear rate of progress led us naturally from the high expectations we had taken for granted to generous praise and applause. I can still see her — feet straddled wide, hands clutching the clips of her coveralls — taking her first real steps. Each new word in her vocabulary became cause for family celebration. Barbara clearly told me of her own awareness of her handicap when she was about five years old and still talking in abbreviated sentences. She was in the kitchen, helping me peel hard-boiled eggs. As she handed me a finished one, I patted her on the head and congratulated her on being a fine kitchen helper. She shook her head and stuck out her lower lip. "You don't want to be a kitchen helper, Barbara?" I asked. "What *do* you want to be when you grow up?" "I wanna read like Karen and David," was her reply. It was a long sentence. I knew then that she was indeed aware of her condition, and that, if we truly respected her as a human being she had the right to frank explanations and discussions of its implications for her later life.

Barbara still cannot really read, although she recognizes many words in her environment — especially the ones that have to do with fast food restaurants and the symbols of many consumer products! She receives much information from television, and that is both helpful and awful, and here at home and at Karen's house she eagerly spends time looking at the many magazines to which we subscribe. I have to remind myself I should read to her more often — both from the printed page and the TV screen.

Regard for differences of opinion was not easy to come by in our family. Al and I agreed on certain basics such as politics, religion and money management, but we disagreed on such sensitive issues as whether claiming a veteran's exemption on our house and land is honorable, and whether hot cereal for breakfast before school is mandatory. We felt strongly we should present a united front to our children on all issues.

One day when Karen was only about five, she startled me by asking the meaning of the word "divorce." "It's when a mummy and daddy don't get along," I tried to explain, "and then maybe they decide not to live in the same house anymore. They fight a lot."

"Like you and Daddy?"

I was appalled." What gives you that idea? We don't fight!"

"You do too!" Karen countered. "Like you say a word is spelled c-a-t and Daddy says c-e-t and then you go and look it up in a book."

David, the product of two parents who had loyally and enthusiastically served in the military during World War II, was an avowed pacifist at age eight. At ten, he caused a heated discussion at the supper table when he challenged the value of daily pledging allegiance to the flag at school. Later he startled us with the question, "Do you think the kids in school in Russia are told that everything is best in their country, too?"

During our children's adolescence, differences of opinion became the order of the day and ranged from hitch-hiking to hotpants, from beards and long hair to booze. The sixties were turbulent years, not without worries or anger, but they prepared us for Barbara's emancipation. First she wanted to grow her hair long like her sister. Then she began to gripe about having to ride on the yellow school bus with all the little kids. Finally she announced in loud and clear tones: "I wanna go somewhere!"

With that Barbara joined the dissonant chorus, and we realized that home is a good place to air your views, be they ever so outrageous. Gradually we learned to hear each other out — to listen and try to accept. As we heard our children's different points of view on all sorts of topics, we learned that they were indeed widely differing people and that their home life was preparing them for an ever-shrinking world full of persons of infinite variety.

Room for differences thus became another component of our family's functioning. As we cheered Barbara for every new skill, we grew in tolerance of each other's short suits. It became acceptable for Mom to be poor at sewing and dense at threading movie projectors at school. Karen was rated as sloppy in the kitchen but an imaginative cook. David's spelling was purely phonetic, but he understood what's under the hood of a car and was an excellent driver. Al encouraged and appreciated this talent — even if it was only around our yard and the house. Father, well Father remained "perfect!"

So our house became known for having space for many and different people, and even now — many years after Al's death — he is remembered in our town as the kindest and most generous of persons. His "open house" attitude spontaneously embraced a young couple he met in the grocery store. They were stranded without accommodations on a drippy, foggy night with only the back seat of their VW Bug for shelter, and they were both tall. He invited them to spend the night in our single-bunk cabin though he had no idea if they were a "sleeping-together-couple." As they pulled out the next morning they thanked us warmly. "I'm an airline stewardess," she turned to me, "and you'd make a good one!"

The drop-out painter with his partner, little boy and new baby stayed for many weeks and contributed to meals by squeezing lots and lots of carrots with their juicer machine. Al finally did ask them to move on.

When Joe the woodcutter and Marie, his wife, lost their cabin to a fire, Al invited them to stay with us. It was a holiday weekend, and our house was already full with our children and friends — college kids, an engineer, and a school teacher. I was irritated by the additional influx, and, looking at the total scene from the perspective of a hostess, it was a strange combination of guests. We were out of spare beds and even the living room floor was full, so Joe and Marie had to roll out sleeping bags in the dining room. I could smell their acrid odor of stale smoke, sweat and booze. Early the next morning I woke up to the sound of an ax on wood. Joe was outside splitting firewood from large redwood rounds and stacking it neatly. This was his trade and the most valuable contribution he could make to our household. I felt warmly grateful to him.

At breakfast Barbara turned to Marie, a woman in her thirties, and asked, "Do you go to school?"

"No," was the answer.

"You can come to my school with me tomorrow," Barbara offered. She had picked up on Marie's condition with deadly accuracy before any of the rest of us had had time to observe it. Marie did not read, and academically she was not very able.

It was this kind of warmth and perception that influenced many of the young people who came to our youth hostel. At times, it did seem like a youth hostel because during Karen's and David's school and college years, both felt free to invite their friends home without making reservations beforehand. In the late sixties I was also beginning to meet members of the Youth California Association for the Retarded, and when they came to "rap," they rolled out their sleeping bags on our living room floor during overflow periods. Having these young people in our home led to a two-way enrichment process. Barbara grew greatly in self-esteem because they made her feel that she was one of them. They, on the other hand, were profoundly moved by her, and a remarkable number chose to enter a field of human services.

I treasure a letter from a young woman who heard me share my concerns for Barbara's future at a meeting of youth delegates at a convention in 1969:

> ...what really brought some tears was when you mentioned Barbara, and who will take care of her if something happens to you. I don't know what happened inside of me, maybe I'm too emotional or something, but I just wanted to come down where you were and say, 'Mrs. Moise, there are lots of people who love Barb, and we won't let anything happen to her.' I guess I'm a little late in expressing the way I felt at the meeting, but I had to 'get it out' cause I can't stand for someone special to feel bad when it comes to the Love of a handicapped child!

Another young friend, Barbara Jessing, grew from a youthful friend on the California scene to an outstanding colleague and an officer of the Youth California Association. When we first met in 1968, she was a college student, working her way through the University of California. She was a counselor at a special summer camp and also had a job in a residential facility. She insisted that she and her fellow members of the youth association did not "serve the retarded," but worked on their behalf and with them. I was on the board of directors of the California Association at the time when she became the first voting youth delegate to this body and I became increasingly impressed with her quiet perseverance and wisdom. The adults in the parent association should have grabbed the wise thoughts and energy of the young people and run with them, for they represented a wonderful potential pool for the work that we had begun. They did not. They missed the boat, and for lack of financial and staff support from the adult board of directors the youth group as an entity faded over the years.

Looking back, though, there was serendipity in this development. The young generation's faith in the potential of our sons and daughters became the seed for the growth of the self-advocacy movement in which persons with developmental disabilities have now become active partners in their life decisions on their own behalf. Some have turned to the field of disabilities as their career choice. I asked Susan (remember my 12-year-old "mainstreaming" tutor?), who now works as a social worker/ case manager in Northern California, if Barbara influenced her decision. This is what she wrote me:

> When I was three years old, in 1958, my family moved to Fort Bragg, California. The Moise family lived down the road a piece and Barbara and I car-pooled to pre-school with various moms and kids. My mother tells me I said many times that I would like to work with people like Barbara when I grew up.
>
> When I was in the eighth grade my dream came true. I 'commuted' on foot the two blocks to the Paul Bunyan School and was a teacher's aide for one period per day. I usually stayed through my lunch hour and loved the time I spent with Barbara and her classmates. That same year I started a volunteer youth group under the umbrella of Parents and Friends to provide social and recreational activities for the 'mentally retarded' children and adults in our community. I

met many fine friends both disabled and non-disabled and continued this volunteer work until I graduated from high school. I also served as a summer camp counselor for developmentally disabled folks during that time and experienced my first grown-up taste of freedom and responsibility away from my home and family.

When my life's journey brought me back to the field of developmental disabilities in 1993 I experienced a true feeling of homecoming. Working as a case manager at the Redwood Coast Regional Center, after being present at the inception of the Regional Center System with Lotte all those years ago, feels like the work I was intended for all my life.

The excitement of our family's trip to Denmark and my follow-up, eye-opening brief stay in Omaha, Nebraska in 1971, turned out to serve as a springboard for three young friends from the ARC youth group. As soon as we returned, Barbara Jessing phoned me. "Don and Paula and I would like to hear about your trip. Would it be okay if we come up the weekend after Thanksgiving?" Of course it was okay. I was as eager to talk about our experiences as they were to hear about them.

"Too bad that you can't afford to fly to Denmark," I said, "but perhaps you could make it to Nebraska next summer." Right then and there we phoned Bob Perske in Omaha where he was directing their parent association. "How would you like some outstanding young volunteers from California next summer? If they can get themselves there on their own, and you give them free room and board in your group homes, they could swing it."

And that's how it happened. The Three Musketeers in two rickety old cars trekked to Nebraska in 1972. Paula, who had graduated with a special teaching credential stayed in Omaha for two years. She returned to California and continued to work with adults with developmental disabilities. Don, a sibling of a young woman with disabilities, returned to finish his degree in sociology in San Francisco. Barbara Jessing still lives in Nebraska — now with a Masters Degree, a family of her own, and work in the social services field. Wherever she lives, persons with developmental disabilities and their parents will continue to be the richer for her presence.

Risk taking was something that Al and I gradually learned to accept as a right of our older children. The first solo ride on a slide, the first night away from home, a bus trip alone, a date with a boy, the driver's license. What made it so much harder to watch Barbara take chances? Perhaps it was that while we had normal expectations of success for Karen and David, Barbara's diagnosis of mental retardation scared us into expecting failure. Once we recognized that risk taking is a prerequisite for learning, we were better able to let go.

So Al taught Barbara to light his pipe and later the fire in the grate. To go on errands to the neighbors and later on the bus by herself. She learned to swim in deep water and to pour hot coffee. Certain learnings, such as crossing busy street corners and riding escalators, we delegated to someone else — someone less personally involved and with a stronger nervous system!

In 1962 David voluntarily undertook one of these risk-taking ventures. I was planning my fourth and last partial summer away from home, this time as a "student professional assistant" at Sonoma State Hospital. Edith Hall had invited our children to come to Fresno for a couple of weeks, but Karen declined. She did not want to leave her beloved horse, Chips, who was a relatively new member of our extended family. Besides, at thirteen she was old enough to try cooking for herself and for her Dad for a while. David and Barbara were dying to go, but we saw no way of getting them there. I was not free to drive them down and Al was loaded with work.

"Do you think that David is old enough to handle this?" Al asked. "He's eleven and pretty hep about transportation," I said, "but I wouldn't want him to feel that he *has* to do it. We could always ask him, though," So we did.

"How would you feel about taking Barbara down to Fresno on the Greyhound with you? It would mean a change in San Francisco and then straight through." David thought a while. "It's okay with me," he said, "except what do I do if she has to go to the bathroom?" That *was* a problem. The total trip would take twelve hours, including the transfer, to get to Fresno. I had nagging doubts. In the San Francisco depot at the time, the women's toilets were up a flight of stairs. A couple of the stalls still had coin slots. This might confuse her. "Well," we told him, "you should probably pick out a motherly looking lady who's going upstairs, and ask her to help your little sister. And then be sure to stay right there so you don't lose her when she comes down." He agreed to do that. Times have changed, and I doubt that I would recommend this procedure today.

Barbara fooled him though. She claimed she didn't have to go in San Francisco and steadfastly maintained the same at every stop on the way south. She performed better than a camel, and poor David, who was unaware of his sister's holding capacity, worried all the way. When they got off the bus in Fresno, Barbara turned to Edith and said, "Hi! I've gotta go wee-wee!"

Al and I sometimes wondered how Karen and David felt about having a little sister with a problem, but we talked to each other about this more than we did with them. Occasionally we made executive decisions about their taking Barbara along with them "because it's only fair"; at other times we asked them, as we did with the Fresno trip.

I asked David how he had felt about his young sister when he was in high school. "It felt a little weird having a sister who was different, but then I felt different anyway when I was in school. Because Karen and I were smart, and too fat, and we weren't part of the 'popular' crowd. Karen wasn't in with the cheerleaders, and I wasn't a football star." But as their parent I know for sure now that we short-changed them by not bringing them together with other siblings of children with disabilities for supportive counseling.

Karen's teenage efforts to establish her identity and independence were more turbulent than those of David, perhaps because she was older and he learned from her mistakes. It hurt to watch her flounder, but with the help of professional counseling, we learned to look at ourselves squarely and our relationships mellowed. Barbara did not seem to be the direct cause of these upsets. We know many families who had no children with special developmental needs who also underwent rebellious teenage times.

When Karen was in her senior year in high school she began to invite Barbara to come along to occasional folk dance recitals and parties. "She's like an icebreaker for me, Mom. I'm lousy at meeting people, but when Barbara is along with me she walks right up, sticks out her hand and introduces herself. 'My name is Barbara,' she'll say. 'What's yours? What did you get for Christmas?' From then on it's easier for me."

During her freshman year at the University of California at Santa Cruz Karen invited Barbara to spend a week with her on campus. At the time it was sort of a free-wheeling campus and she was safely stashed away with her sleeping bag in Karen's room. She could join her sister in some classes and seminars. At other times she stayed in the dorm, listened to records, and visited up and down the hall. The entire floor of students looked after her. Two years later — not to be outdone — David also wanted her to spend a week with him. This time he and his roommate improvised a temporary sleeping loft in their beamed, high-ceilinged room. They both slept on this platform while Barbara was down below. She returned home from each of these visits more alert than before, with a noticeable increase in self-motivation and a rush of new words and concepts.

It was on one of these Santa Cruz trips that we first became aware of Barbara's extraordinary sixth sense. In 1968, when she was fourteen and David seventeen, we asked David to pick up his sister at the end of her stay with Karen. He was proud owner of a hard- earned car and glad of every opportunity to drive it. Grandma Mud was living in Fort Bragg by then, and at almost ninety, she was a little frail. That weekend a friend had invited Al, Mud and me to dinner. During dinner she suddenly looked uneasy. Her left hand wouldn't hold anything and one side of her face looked droopy. We took her home, helped her to bed and called the doctor. It was a very mild stroke, he said, not much more severe than the light fainting spells she'd had from time to time. "Stay in bed tomorrow, Mud," he ordered, "and don't worry about your hand. Two or three days of rest and you'll be as good as new."

When David and Barbara rolled in that Sunday evening, the first words out of Barbara's mouth were, "What's the matter with Mud? Is Mud okay?" I was too startled to answer. It lightly crossed my mind that the two might have stopped by to see her on the way home. Then David popped out on the driver's side and said, "Is anything the matter with Mud, Mom? All the way home Barbara has been bugging me about Mud — worrying how she is!"

There have been other times when Barbara seemed to know about something that happened when she wasn't physically present. This capacity seems to have faded over the years. I have a hunch (not a proven scientific theory) that we have tried to fill her head with facts and figures of daily living, thus crowding out this fine "sixth sense" that we know so little about. I have wondered about the possibility that persons with so-called mental retardation might have more highly developed extrasensory perception than the rest of us. At one time I was sorely tempted to study at the respected Jung Institute in Zurich, where scholars have done impressive studies on ESP, but the uphill push for community programs here in California has had to come first.

We blundered and wondered a lot during the risk-taking teenage years of our three children. Of course we worried about Barbara. We worried that someone might hurt her feelings, cheat her when she shopped, or take advantage of her trusting affection. But we also recognized that we cannot let our worry become her straitjacket. We must not cheat her of her right to failure, which is as integral a component of growth as is success.

I once heard the most damning indictment of parents uttered by a young woman with severe physical disabilities. "Disabled persons are the one oppressed minority," she said, "where the parents tend to be on the side of the oppressors." I believe that parents can do better than this. That we can and should become our sons' and daughters' allies and advocates in their striving for independence. Slowly this is happening as American society is becoming aware of the worth of its disabled fellow citizens and their rightful access to fair and equal opportunities and supports. It has taken grass roots *and* federal efforts like the Americans With Disabilities Act to begin to give us hope.

RESPONSIBILITY became an "all-cap" word in our household — almost to a fault. It applied to daily school attendance, Sunday School, Cub Scout meetings, and concerts. To Al and me a promise meant a total commitment, and we expected our children to abide by our standards of responsibility. In desperation David once turned to his father and burst out, "But what if I don't want to grow up to be as good as you, Dad!" With that we began to realize that a sense of responsibility cannot be dictated. Everyone must experience the consequences of his or her actions and learn from the consequences.

We felt strongly that Barbara also learn responsible and appropriate behavior in the framework of our home, and gradually she did. She was clumsily destructive at first. Favorite trucks lost wheels. Dolls were decapitated and even expensive orthopedic shoes disappeared and set us on combing tall grass all around the house. It was difficult to act as referee between an irate older brother or sister, both of whom tried to take care of their possessions, and Barbara, who was exploring with a vengeance. Later she learned to leave their things alone, and although she still tends to probe the innards of her transistor radio, she is pretty organized with her belongings.

No secret formula aided this learning process. She was exposed to the same group dynamics as her brother and sister were. We praised and scolded, rewarded and punished, hugged, and even occasionally spanked. We learned that many concepts needed to be explained to Barbara with greater patience and repeated more often. We still catch her at times giving "flip" incorrect answers instead of telling the truth. I believe it is because a brief answer requires less effort than a long sentence. And she is so honest that it is difficult for her to understand the difference between a white lie, which is socially acceptable and sometimes necessary, and a serious falsehood.

Becoming responsible involves many, many steps which are hard for anyone to take, and positive presumptions used to be whisked away from parents at the first mention of the big bad words "mental retardation." Then, with the rug pulled out from under them, parents were scared into expecting failure, and their expectations would mushroom into a fear of almost everything else. We "over-handicapped" our children by definition. As a result we began to make decisions *for* our children instead of giving them choices. Al and I slowly learned that this applied to Barbara as well. Only by being presented with choices — be they ever so small and seemingly insignificant — can any child learn responsible behavior.

"Choice," according to Webster, "is the voluntary act of selecting or separating from two or more things that which is preferred." We let Barbara "select" when she came to restaurants with us (yes, we stared down the starers), and we encouraged her to order from a menu, though we had to read it to her. When the waiter invariably turned to Al or me and asked: "and what does *she* want?" we'd counter with, "Why don't you ask her?" The restaurants with picture menus became her favorites!

There were unfortunate occasions, which I remember with embarrassment, when I was the one who put obstacles in the way of her "voluntary act of selecting that which is preferred." When Barbara announced that she wanted to grow her hair long like Karen's, I told her, "No! You look very nice with short hair, and it's a lot of work to take care of it when it's long. You have to rinse it a whole lot more when you wash it, and you'd have a hard time putting it up in curlers. No! Wait until you're bigger." As far as I was concerned the subject was closed, but our girl persisted. As soon as Karen heard of the fuss, she went to bat for Barbara. "Why not, Mother? Why shouldn't she? Everybody is wearing their hair long these days." I gave in reluctantly, and for several years Barbara wore her hair long and managed to take care of it.

Another time we were shopping for a new outfit. Barbara tried on several slacks and tops, and we had narrowed down the choice to some gray flannel pants with a matching sweater and a dark red pantsuit which was identical with a bright green one she had chosen the year before. She looked pretty in either outfit, but I thought it was boring to have two suits just alike and said so. In fact I really tried to talk her into the slacks and sweater. "But I like the red one," she said, "and it feels comfortable." With that we bought the one she preferred.

To learn to let her choose clothes and food was relatively easy and painless. Other choices were more difficult, and often I completely missed the cues she gave me. I blushingly remember one such incident when her tenth birthday was approaching. She and I were making a list of friends to invite to her party and she wanted to invite just about everyone in her school, and Susan too. Susan was the little neighbor girl with whom she had gone to nursery school. Now Barbara was going to the Paul Bunyan School, and Susan to regular public elementary school. Susan had come to all of Barbara's previous birthday parties, but for some reason I thought that she might have outgrown Barbara and her friends so I talked her out of asking Susan.

It was Susan's mom who set me straight. "Didn't Barbara have a birthday the other day?" she asked me when we ran into each other in town," and didn't she have a party this year?" I explained that I had persuaded Barbara not to include Susan because I had been afraid that she might not want to come. "You shouldn't have done that," she said. "Susan really cares about Barbara." Thoughtlessly I had overridden one of Barbara's decisions. Because I was afraid of a potentially uncomfortable situation for our girl, I came close to depriving her of the opportunity of a friendship. Barbara knew that Susan liked her, but I had not listened. We soon mended that fence, and she and Susan care about each other to this day.

The following words were written by a ten-year old Swiss girl after a mother went to her class to speak about her daughter's problem of mental retardation. The teacher then asked his students for a report. Isabelle wrote the following (translated):

> Retarded children are those who do not have a good memory, but they have a lot of heart. When you have a retarded friend, you can leave him for five years, and he will recognize you and come right to you. It is not his intelligence which comes towards you, but his heart which sees your heart and recognizes it.

Readiness for role changes is the sixth and possibly the most difficult R to attain. The ups and downs of childhood and maturity are strangely unpredictable. The transition from childhood and dependence rarely happens smoothly. Yesterday our children piled into bed with us to snuggle. Today they pull away from hugs and kisses. Small bids for adult status become a big deal and alternate with regression into childish tantrums, but overall most children dream of becoming grown-ups and children with special needs are no different.

Barbara longed for the status symbol of female maturity, her monthly period, when she was only eleven. When she was older, her non-driver identification card from the Department of Motor Vehicles, complete with photo, was a source of great pride to her. With Karen and David we had expected adulthood, but with Barbara it took jolt after small jolt to shake us out of our overprotective parental attitude.

One day Barbara complained of a headache. "Want to take an aspirin?" I asked. "I already did," she replied, and with that I jumped all over her. "Don't you remember," I roared," that we have a rule in this house that you *never* take any medicine without asking?" Her lower lip drooped. "But I know aspirin," and she quickly led me to the medicine cabinet and showed me the bottle. The thought suddenly occurred to me that our daughter was eighteen and a young adult. We were thinking of letting her move into a group home, and I couldn't unlearn my "smother" role. I apologized to her. "We have a new rule now — a rule for young adults who know aspirin," I told her.

Another time, during her teenage years, Al and I assumed that she would go to a community concert with us. "I'm not going," she announced that evening. "Oh yes, you are. We've got season tickets, and you're coming with us." I was still afraid to leave her home alone in the evening, although we lived on a safe country road and had a good dog. Even so I pressured her longer. Finally she burst out in exasperation, "I hate that kind of music (classical) and I want my peace." With this outburst she overcame our apprehension, and she accomplished her small bid for independence by a clear bit of communication. She asked for a quiet evening at home, and for a change we listened.

There is another aspect of this growing up process — and I mean hers and mine and other families of children with developmental problems. We need to think of the reality of sickness be it sudden or chronic, life threatening or less serious. Sickness is also a part of life, and it may require a stay in the hospital and can be a scary experience unless we prepare for it. It is a two-way learning experience for children and adults with special needs and the staffs of hospitals and nursing homes.

Barbara had such an experience at an early age and spent a day and a night in the hospital. I was taking her temperature one day when she bit down on the thermometer by mistake. It broke, and though I rescued both ends of it, I couldn't be 100 percent sure that she had not swallowed a bit of mercury. "Bring her down," said our doctor and tried to get her to vomit. It didn't work, and she had to pump out her stomach, and then suggested that she be admitted so that she could watch her. "I'm almost certain that she'll be okay, but wouldn't this be a fine occasion to introduce her to a hospital experience?" I nodded yes. "How would you like to stay with us until tomorrow, Barbara? Just to make sure your tummy is all right?"

Barbara beamed from ear to ear. "Stay overnight?" And then, "Pack me a suitcase, Mom."

She knew exactly what she wanted in it too! She lay in the six-bed ward like the Queen of the May and enjoyed all the friendly service. The nurses commented that she was such a good girl, and so cooperative. When we picked her up the following morning, she cried a little.

We followed up on this small adventure a couple of years later, when a friend of mine was teaching a course for licensed vocational nurses. We agreed that all of our students at the Paul Bunyan School ought to be prepared for a possible hospital stay, and her nursing students would also benefit from getting to know our students. The class for the nurses-in-training took place right across the street and so we were able to introduce the children to hospital beds, bedpans, urinals, emesis basins, and hypodermic needles. The instructor even volunteered to have an injection of distilled water. As she pulled the needle out of her arm, I heard one of our youngsters say, "Hey! You didn't even cry!" I wish I could say that Barbara learned from this part of the lesson. She is still scared stiff of shots and of all intrusive procedures and I wish I could say she is an easy patient. She is not.

By the time Barbara was about twelve, the age at which most hospitals permit children to visit patients, we began taking her along with us to see sick friends. She had learned not to be afraid of our friend Jack's seizures. The first time he had one at our house, Barbara bluntly asked him to leave. "Go away!" she said. "Go to your house." She was acting out of fear rather than rudeness. As we talked with her she learned to accept Jack's condition. Later, when he was hospitalized and slowly dying from a brain tumor, Barbara knew it. She vacillated between fear of seeing him close to death and wanting to visit him because she loved him. When she came along with us he made her smile with his brave humor. "Jack isn't sad," she commented.

As a child she seemed able to handle the deaths of our pets with more equanimity than I. There were dogs and cats that were run over and we all grieved for them. One time a neighbor phoned to tell me that she thought one of our cats had been hit and was lying on the road nearby. I went to pick it up. It looked pretty messy, so I carried it gingerly by the tail and put it just inside our driveway for Al to bury later. Barbara was home and cried just a little when I told her. Then she went to see for herself, and when I looked out of the window I was amazed to see her less afraid of handling the cat than I had been. She cradled it gently in her arms and talked to it softly. First she put it down in one place, and then another until she found a soft grassy spot close to the house. She came inside, washed her hands, and said, "That's better. This evening Al bury her."

Wally was an especially beloved dachshund. He too was hit by a car and died during the night. We all got dressed early that morning so that we could help Al with Wally's burial before school. Except Barbara. She was still poking around in her bathrobe, looking sad. "Come on, Barb, don't you want to come out and help Daddy bury Wally?" we urged her. She shook her head. "Why not? What do you want to do?"

"Can't we make a rug out of Wally?" was her wistful reply.

I met a new member of one of our state's Regional Center's board of trustees some years ago. I was introduced to him with the statement, "Mrs. Moise has a daughter with mental retardation." I shook his hand and welcomed him.

"How'd you do," he said, and added, "Sometimes I wish I were re-tarded too. They're always so happy." I recovered in time to tell that man that he was underestimating our sons and daughters and that they are people who know the full range of human emotions.

Later I asked myself if we actually do let our children experience the full range of emotions. How can we honestly interpret their total humanness to others, if we, their parents, are less than honest with them? And honesty includes our preparing them for sickness and dy-ing. They deserve no less than that. It should be the underpinning for cohesive families so that our sons and daughters will be able to live "in the middle of things" as Bob Perske says, "where they belong."

Barbara wrapping a gift

Barbara watering the plants in the garden at Penngrove, 1977

Barbara with long hair

Chapter 10

Coming of Age

Coming of age when you have a disability is tough. For Barbara it really began with our trip to Denmark in 1971.

Our entire family took a giant step forward in our perception of fine programs for persons with disabilities and our awareness of the growth potential of those who live in such programs. David became involved by osmosis. During our stay in Denmark Al promised that his shop, Redwood Coast Printers, would print my required report — even photos. I wanted other parents to share our exciting experience. David was put in charge of the project which resulted in a slim illustrated booklet called *See How They Grow!* which I sent to hundreds of friends and co-workers on our return.

Barbara took naturally to all the new experiences. The day after our arrival in Copenhagen we visited the group home that was to be the core of my study. It was a comfortable three-story brick house on a quiet residential street between two busy boulevards. Twelve young women (it has since become a co-ed residence) lived there with their director, three trained care assistants, a full-time cook/housekeeper and a handyman. Elna Skov, the director, glowed with warmth and enthusiasm. "We would like you to spend some time with us while you are here, Barbara," she told our youngest. "When?" was our daughter's instant reply. We returned to the hotel right then and there to help her pack a small suitcase, and Barbara moved in that day. She spent an entire month at the residence so that I was able to observe and record the goal-setting, striving, and "stretching," which were an integral part of Denmark's "normalization" process and affected my own daughter's life.

As Al, Karen and I walked back to our hotel in the evening of the first day, we asked ourselves the big question, "How come these girls don't look or act 'retarded'?" A month later we had soaked up enough new concepts, challenging ideas, and food for thought for years to come.

Because Barbara was only a temporary resident and did not know the language, it was decided that she would assist with work around the house instead of "working out" like the other young women. "But," said Elna, turning to Al, "she should learn to walk back and forth to your hotel. You could teach her. First show her the way. Then follow to see that she does it right until she can do it alone."

It was a fifteen minute walk. Our small town girl had to cross two major boulevards with strange looking traffic lights (Fort Bragg had only two traffic lights in 1971), and she gave her nervous father a couple of scary moments. The first time he walked just a few steps behind her. At corners she would turn around, check for his okay, and then cross alone. The next time he hung back a good distance and let her make her own decision. Sure enough she goofed. He saw her turn left down the big street instead of crossing at the corner. Suddenly she noticed her mistake, but — oh horror! — instead of backtracking to the corner with the signal, she raised her hand like a policeman directing traffic, and struck out across the street right in the middle of the block. Al almost had heart failure, but all the speedy little Danish cars stopped in time! Soon she no longer needed anyone's protection. Had she been a regular resident, she would then have been taught a bus route to her place of work.

Shopping came next. I had to admit to Elna that only once in her entire life had Barbara bought a pair of knee socks for herself, all by herself. Elna's residents gradually learned to purchase everything they needed independently. Much staff time was expended to teach them about quality, good value and good style. They took great pride in their purchases and appearance, and without exception everyone looked neat, stylish, and appropriately dressed. I asked Elna if she and her staff would write a program for Barbara "as if she were a Danish girl entering as a new resident." She looked at me quizzically and asked, "Might not your feelings be hurt, Mother?" I assured her that I could take it, and she and her assistants promptly sat down with Barbara and prepared a one-month program:

- Not to suck her thumb.
- To keep shoulders back.
- Not to laugh too loud or without motivation.
- To sit down on chairs gently and in a ladylike manner.
- To eat less noisily at the table.
- To keep her blouse all the way out or in.
- To arrange the collar of her jacket neatly.

The goals were simple, straightforward, and attainable. All of us — Barbara, staff persons, and family — evaluated her progress at the end of the month.

We began to respect the idea of risk taking which Bob Perske had experienced and vividly described in his travel reports. It was obvious that Barbara's balance and mobility were improving. (Sadly she has experienced setbacks in recent years.) In the house in Copenhagen her room was on the third floor. At home in California our fearful girl hardly ever needed to walk up and down stairs. Our house was the one-story ranch style variety. Here she was learning to negotiate the narrow winding staircase to her room and before the month was over she could do it without holding on to the banister, even while carrying something in her hands. It was simply taken for granted that she would learn. For many young people in Danish programs, risk taking was part of work situations in which the use of carefully "jigged" expensive power tools required concentration and resulted in great poise. We also noted that continued education motivated them to strengthen their independent living skills.

Money was spent generously on many programs. Persons who were unable to walk were provided with therapy and equipment to put them on their feet. Furnishings in state residences and in community group homes were almost luxurious by our standards. They seemed to say, "Nothing is too good for you," and the young women and men who lived surrounded by such beauty grew in pride and care for their possessions.

We soon realized that excellent and continuing staff training — both academic and hands-on — for front line personnel — was one of the secrets of success for programs and residents. Working in the field of disabilities was a respected career. Salaries and benefits conformed to a national norm both for institutional and community workers in vocational and residential programs alike. There were opportunities for staff persons to advance to supervisory and administrative positions if they so chose.

By 1971 I had already experienced working in one of California's institutions. Denmark also still had state residences but they were very different and by the nature of the country much smaller. There is one particular impression that I have always carried with me. In one of these Danish residences the son of the Director was a photographer, and the walls in the hallways were decorated with pictures that he had taken of the young men who lived there. I had seen and met them and they were without exception visibly and severely multiply disabled. He had caught their beauty and humanity. They all looked handsome! And each one treasured a key to his own room. It was clear that the positive, dynamic attitudes of the staff reflected directly on residents, increasing their self-confidence and enhancing their self-concept.

The Danes too were concerned with the issue of parental overprotection. I was apparently not the only mother in the world who bought all her teenage daughter's clothes for her. Elna told me of mothers who answered for their children, pre-empted their every decision, and never discussed with them the implications of their condition on their adult life in the community.

As I sorted through and assessed my experiences, one thought surfaced that depressed me. How could I ever "sell" all these beautiful concepts at home? "Of course," people would snort, "That's what you get in a socialist country." It happened otherwise.

I had promised Bob Perske, newly arrived in Omaha, Nebraska, to direct the Greater Omaha Association for the Retarded, that I would stop and report on my experiences. "I think I'm too tired to come, Bob," I said when I phoned him from New York. "Besides, I have a cold, and next week is Thanksgiving. Al and the girls are on their way home and I'm anxious to get there too."

"I wish you'd come, Lotte," he said earnestly." I really wish you'd take a couple of extra days to see what's happening here. This is even more exciting than Denmark." With that he brought me up short. Coming from the man who had first introduced me to all the exciting Scandinavian normalization ideas, it had to be true.

And it was. It was actually happening in conservative, corn belt Nebraska. ENCOR, the Eastern Nebraska Community Office of Retardation, was putting together a comprehensive, community based program for children and adults, which included former institutional residents and children with severe multiple developmental disabilities. It was happening under the leadership of three men with a vision. One was an eminent University Professor of Pediatrics, one a philosopher-ethicist, and Perske the agency executive. The young staff persons were enthusiastic and energetic and I forgot all about my cold as they ran me through their homes, apartments, workshops and work stations in industry from early morning to the small hours of the night — usually winding up with beer in a bowling alley! I no longer needed to be depressed about our country's long distance from Denmark and socialism. We could make good programs happen here at home.

It was high time, because, though Al and I were not too surprised to observe signs of restlessness and rebellion with Karen and David, we had not expected Barbara to "come of age" after we returned from the Dybwad fellowship in Denmark. But she did.

Again she started the process. After eleven years of going to school in the same little old house on a quiet side street, with the same teachers and the same small group of fellow students day in and day out, she began to rebel. "I wanna go somewhere!" she complained as I shoved her onto the school bus she used to love. Once, in a crazy moment of frustration, as I watched her wave a sad goodbye to Karen and

David as they took off for college, I asked: "How would you like to go back to Denmark to live?"

"They don't talk right." was her reply.

Her new school in Marin County, a four-hour drive away, was a tremendous stimulant. From a program of twelve children of all ages, she went to a school with fifty young adults. The school had a pre-vocational program — a precursor to our attempts at "transitioning" in the California public schools of today. There was a shop equipped with power tools where students made wooden objects. They took care of small animals and hired out as a crew to do gardening work. Some learned photography and simple duplicating. Barbara took particular pride in her ceramics, and she loved the choir and rhythm band. For the first time in her life our daughter had a chance to perform before a large group of parents and guests in the assembly program that concluded the school year.

The occasion did not exactly result in undiluted pride and glory. Al took off from work and we drove south on a sunny Saturday afternoon to share her joy. The auditorium was filled with about two hundred proud parents and friends. There were speeches by special education administrators and presentations of diplomas and special honors for the graduates. And then came the entertainment by the rhythm band and the choir. Barbara was one of the singers. She had spotted us in the audience, and as her excitement mounted, it also increased the volume of her voice to a full crescendo. One of her more experienced schoolmates noticed her blast and gave her a slight nudge in the ribs, whereupon our daughter turned around and gave her the finger in full view of the audience! It was spontaneous but totally inappropriate. She was bawled out for it, and we hope she has learned that obscene gestures get one into trouble.

Finding a suitable home was the difficulty. Even as late as 1972 in the sophisticated Bay Area community it was difficult. We could never have accomplished it without the help of a fellow mother who had years of experience advocating for her daughter, but it turned out to be a disaster.

Barbara's weekend reports about the home into which she moved were guarded. It was brand new, shiny and clean, and the caretaker came with solid references from a previous position in a similar home. Barbara had one housemate. All seemed to be going well, but then she mentioned the housemother's drinking too much. "We went to the bar," she told us, "and I had a diet coke." We thought it might be Barbara's immature way of getting back at the new authority figure who was making her toe the line and do her chores, but did decide to confront the woman. We were as tactful as possible. She assured us that all was under control.

That summer Barbara spent a long, happy vacation with us at home, and she was full of enthusiasm to move back when school started. Her housemother looked great. She had trimmed down by losing twenty pounds, and we were at ease until the crisis hit us. Barbara had been right. There *was* a drinking problem.

One evening the housemother went out on a binge and brought her drunken boyfriend home. She herself passed out in the hallway, and he molested our daughter. We have never been able to find out from Barbara exactly what happened, but we know that it was a traumatic sexual experience. She has since become much more frightened of intrusive medical procedures like pelvic exams which are routinely necessary for young women. It was a nightmarish experience, especially for me, and it challenged all my beliefs and convictions. I wanted to wrap her up and bring her home!

We took no legal action against the caretaker at the time. The woman lost her license and I have no idea what happened to her. Barbara was able to finish the school year in the home of the parents of a classmate. It was her own choice to continue in school, and we all — our entire family and theirs — stood by her staunchly and closely for the rest of the year.

For me it became a "red alert" and I have become acutely vigilant about the existence of abuse — especially sexual abuse — as a danger for our sons and daughters who live in the community. Abuse does *not* only happen in large institutions, and we know it.

There now exist many studies about sexual abuse to prove that young persons with special developmental needs are especially vulnerable, and the perpetrators range from friends and relatives to caretakers and school bus drivers. It puts us, the parents on a two-edged sword, as we fight like tigers for their right to be included in the real world just like their siblings, while we fear for them and would rather keep them in our protective kangaroo pouch.

Over the past twenty years we have made inroads into the legal system. While we try to publicly deal with spousal and elder abuse, we are also beginning to look at the prevalence of danger to our sons and daughters, and how to help them through such trauma. Here on the West Coast, Nora Baladerian, Ph.D., heads a Disability, Abuse & Personal Rights Project called *Spectrum Institute*. She teaches and writes about interviewing skills to use with abuse victims who have developmental disabilities, and who were heretofore not considered capable of communicating what happened to them in an abuse situation. She works and lectures with police and courts.

Our family should have advocated more militantly for Barbara during that trauma. Today we are better equipped to assist our children safely through adolescence into adulthood.

It was the summer of 1973. California's network of regional counseling and diagnostic centers was complete and functioning by the time the school year ended. Our own rural area of four northern counties was still under-served, but we were finally funded by the legislature and one of the last to complete the network of thirteen Advocacy Area Boards and twenty-one Regional Centers. Barbara now had a case manager, and we, her parents, a counselor. So we turned to them for help in finding a new place to live for our adult-to-be.

Again a trial visit was arranged, this time to a large facility in the Bay Area which reminded Barbara of "Elna's house" (the group home in Copenhagen). Both Karen and David lived near by — Karen in Nursing School and David working as a printer and studying for his A.A. at a Community College. So Barbara became a city dweller.

We had confidence in the general direction and philosophy of the house, and it certainly reassured us that David and Karen were so close to her. Both of them had grown into observant, responsible advocates for their sister, and she spent as much time with them as possible.

It was the journey home that became a worry to us all. Barbara was not afraid of riding the Greyhound Bus, but we worried on every one of her travel days. Her house staff people took her to the bus. They helped her buy the ticket. At the main depot in San Francisco she had to change — and wait! She knew the number of her bus and could read the words Fort Bragg, *but* the depot was not a choice spot for security. Over the years most Greyhound stations seem to have slipped into the least desirable neighborhoods of many cities. Available, safe, public transportation has continued to be a major issue and concern for disability advocates.

With Barbara we talked about it over and over. We rehearsed and role played situations that might occur. I pretended to be a handsome young man who approached her. "Say, good looking, where are you going?" I'd say.

"Fort Bragg."

"Geez! you don't want to wait all that time. I've got a car. I'm going to Eureka. I'll drive you there." Then I'd ask "and what are you going to do then, Barbara? Are you going with him?" I was relieved every time she negotiated the trip safely, and luckily she always did.

When Karen and David moved to Southern California it made a huge difference in her level of satisfaction. She no longer looked forward to returning to the city. We began to wonder. She was regaining weight. Her workshop assignment was "DD deadly dull." She was unfolding newspapers for hours on end. She became bratty and was terminated. We also heard her complain about the house: "It's too big! Too far! There's nothing to do!" She was telling us loud and clear that she was unhappy. As we were driving off the freeway towards her house one day she said, "Ugly, ugly city? What am I doing down here?" That did it.

Once again we began to prepare for a move, but this time we had help. It was not an easy task to find a quality home closer to home. One of the best was located in our county seat, but once more the transportation problem loomed. There was none, and Barbara would have to depend on our driving her back and forth for visits. Looking well into the future I could see how Al and I might find it difficult to manage that hour and a half curvy drive each way on foggy, rainy weekend nights. Sonoma County — one county further south — offered two possibilities, and there *was* a once-a-day direct Greyhound bus connection.

Her new counselor was helpfully understanding. When he found two small group homes that seemed well staffed and programmed for increasing their residents' skills in daily living, he arranged for Barbara to spend a long weekend trying the two places. She would stay overnight first in one house and then in the other. She'd also visit a couple of near-by work activity centers that might have openings for her. Then the counselor would drive her back to the city so they'd have time to talk about Barbara's impressions. She had a month to make a decision and Al and I promised we'd let her talk, and we would listen and stay out of it as much as possible.

And she did talk about it. One day she came into the room where I was typing and sat quietly close to my desk. I could almost hear the wheels go around in her head. "What's the matter?" I asked her.

"I'm nervous," she said.

"Worried about moving?"

"Yes, I'll miss my friends," she replied with tears in her eyes. I moved close to her and hugged her. I shared her sadness at parting, but I was delighted that she really was weighing the pros and cons of this big decision. I let her tell me about the two houses that she had seen, and then we talked about missing friends, and I assured her that we would help her to stay in touch.

I hadn't really thought about this before. It's so easy for most of us to nurture friendships with a letter or a long distance call. We can hop into our cars and arrange for a weekend visit. Barbara doesn't have all these options. A young woman who had been a member of California's youth advocacy group and gone on to become a staff person in a day activity program, echoed my feelings: "I'm tired of trying to teach my students to balance their checkbooks which they may or may not

123

ever need. I'd rather teach them how to buy a birthday card to send to a friend."

Barbara's move was a good one. It was a small group home in a semi-rural area, closer to us and with bus connections. It came under the umbrella of SCILS (Sonoma County Independent Living Skills). Barbara was the first woman to move into the residence with four young men — a situation which may well have influenced her decision. We were pleased, though her integration process seemed slow in the beginning. It seems that one of the highlights of Barbara's trial-run visit had been that the young men had asked her to join them on their customary Friday evening out for supper. They had gone to McDonalds — at the time Barbara's absolute favorite dining establishment. Three Fridays passed, and they didn't ask her again. Barbara didn't seem to be concerned but her house counselor and I wondered what the problem was. On the fourth Friday it became clear. Barbara's SSI (Supplemental Social Security) check caught up with her from the other county, and then they asked her to come along.

Barbara blossomed in her new surroundings. We had hoped that this would happen, but didn't expect to see the change happen so fast. The nearness to Karen had much to do with it. Karen had moved to Sonoma County to complete her studies for a degree and a family nurse practitioner certification and was living two miles down the road. They saw each other often.

It was not just Karen, though, or the closer and simpler bus connection to our house. There were other reasons, both tangible and intangible for the improved quality of her life. In her new situation the small-group principle prevailed. The house may have been "funky" but the atmosphere was relaxed and essentially a gathering of individuals who lived together. Outings were spontaneous — not highly organized field trips, but just something one chooses to do for the afternoon or evening. A local bus stopped near by and she could walk to the store. She was learning new skills at her work center and saved her small check stubs proudly to show them off to us.

I especially liked the way the program consultant planned for each resident individually. I saw her do her work right at the kitchen table, surrounded by supper preparations and unfazed by the confusion. There were no hierarchical distinctions between the social work staff, the house staff and the residents. "We/they" lines between staff and residents were refreshingly absent. On my visits I felt welcomed as a parent/advocate. I could drop in anytime and was encouraged to make suggestions for my daughter's program or welfare. Soon after Barbara had settled at Penngrove House Karen wrapped up the situation in one sentence: "The difference is that they really like Barbara here."

Many of the staff persons were college students and were not earning a generous salary. Yet they worked hard and there was a spirit of teamwork in the house. Each resident was helped to meet the specific goals of his or her program plan, and quarterly reports were passed to the regional center counselor, the work activity center, and to the parents and guardians. Barbara showed improvement in cooking skills and in doing her own laundry. Part of the report dealt with her earnest efforts at regulating her diet, her thumb-sucking abatement program, and an update on any physical or medical problems that needed attention. We really felt secure in knowing what was going on with our daughter.

The changes in Barbara began to show up soon. On one of her first weekend visits at home she appeared more animated, sat up taller, and had more to say to us about all sorts of happenings. And she volunteered to help. She stood in the kitchen, saying "Can I do the dishes?" proudly, and when she dug out the shoeshine kit and announced that she was going to clean her boots, I couldn't believe my eyes. It had been a long time since those boots had been shined.

There were other landmark indications of growth in independence. She seemed to change from a docile little girl to one who occasionally spoke up politely and firmly. On one of my visits to her house she invited me to have supper with them. I watched her pile butter on the baked potato and mayonnaise on the artichoke and quietly mumbled a few warning words to her from across the table. She looked me squarely in the eye and put me right in my place. "This is my house!" she said. It happened here at home too. Barbara had just come home for a weekend and we had guests for dinner. I asked her to take the soup bowls off the table and into the kitchen. "I'm not your maid," was her smiling reply as she got up and did it.

She had to overcome bumps in her new road. Early one morning my phone rang and her counselor told me she had slipped and fallen as she took the local bus to work. The driver had pulled out a bit too fast as she was getting on too slowly. "She's okay," he said, "just a bruise on her shin. And she wanted to go on to work. We thought you should know, though." Of course she was scared, but she valiantly continued riding the bus.

When I asked her if she could tell me why she liked living at Penngrove House she said, "I like the boys — and we ride the bus." The bus — in contrast to the special van — was definitely a symbol of independence for her.

Once more Barbara's new living situation became a learning experience of the highest order. I became more and more convinced that we *must* give our hands-on front line staff persons opportunities for training, and decent salaries with benefits, so that their work with our sons and daughters — whether in their residential homes or work places — can lead to a secure and fulfilling career.

I wish I could say that now — twenty years later — we have solved the economic problems of community living. We have not. The chasm between salaries and benefits for staff persons who work for the State of California, either in institutions (development centers as we call them), the twenty-one Regional Centers, or the Department of Developmental Services in Sacramento, and those in local community programs is still abysmal.

From time to time we have mounted efforts to bring fairness into the now overblown bureaucratic system we created with the best of intentions. In 1991 two state assembly members introduced such a bill. Out in the field we referred to it as "The Fairness Bill." It addressed the wage disparities between employees in state facilities and private programs.

Existing law requires the State Department of Developmental Services to establish and maintain an equitable system of payment to providers of services to persons with developmental disabilities in community living facilities and other programs.

The Fairness Bill did not ask for immediate funding, but rather for "a plan regarding the achievement of wage fairness standards by these providers over a period not to exceed five years."

The Governor vetoed the bill for the following reason:

> Typically, individuals residing in development centers (state institutions) are substantially more medically fragile and behaviorally disabled than persons living in the community, and are consequently more demanding. In order to provide for the needs of such individuals, the staff of development centers must have more training and must for the most part be licensed in one or more health professions. The same is not true of the staff of community facilities.

So it did not happen. Five years later the natives are restless again. State employees receive cost of living increases with some regularity, while community programs must strain to cover their budget short-falls with fundraising efforts. We lose dedicated staff persons to more remunerative positions, and that is a wrenching experience for them and a great loss to our programs. Repeatedly in the past many years, when a beloved person in her house changed jobs, Barbara has expressed her sense of loss. While she doesn't understand the intricacies of budgets, she picks up on the underlying cause. "They need more money for me," I've heard her say. Or, "Our house needs more money." Each time it's like a betrayal of Barbara, who worries but has no control over changing the situation.

Chapter 11

The Touchy Subject of Sexuality

One day when my good friend and volunteer Eleanor Melville took Barbara to the grocery store, she ran right into the need for a basic lesson in the facts of life. They wheeled their purchases to the check-out counter, and in the line right behind them was a man with a pot belly hanging way out over his belt. Eleanor noticed Barbara's eyes riveted on the man's stomach. She could feel her question brewing, and out it came: "Are you going to have a baby?"

The checker sputtered with laughter. The fat man took it good-naturedly, and Eleanor explained that babies grow only in women's stomachs. She told me about the incident when I came to pick up Barbara, and though we didn't dwell on it then, it went down as one of the many markers on the road towards recognizing my child's interest in sexuality and rightful need for information.

My fears about her womanhood stemmed from the time when she was a year and a half old, and we had first had to confront the outspoken diagnosis of mental retardation. I had asked our close friend and family physician, "What will happen when Barbara matures, Lloyd? Will men take advantage of her? Do you think she'll ever be able to marry and have children?"

This kind and thoughtful man tried to set my mind at ease by saying, "You've got a lot of time, Lotte, and in your home I can see no reason why she should not be able to learn the difference between right and wrong."

It was an old-fashioned answer. Almost a no answer to an impossible question. As gently as he could, Lloyd shifted the responsibility onto our family's shoulders. Right then I made up my mind that sex would have no place in Barbara's life. Just how I expected to accomplish this, however, was still unclear. I had too many other concerns that were more pressing. The fact that I did was fortunate, for I had time to observe and think — and learn.

The changes did not take place in any logical, lock-step sequence. First I had to work through my own experience and come to grips with the differences in Al's and my own sexual attitudes. Our attitudes and taboos were somewhat different. Mine were perhaps more open and less puritanical in theory, but less advanced than his in action. My physician father who, as a dermatologist specialized in sexually transmitted diseases, answered my teenage questions openly. I remember asking Papi about premarital relationships. His advice went something like this: "I really think that up to the age of about twenty-one, a girl is better off not experimenting with sex, because it can get into sticky situations both physically and emotionally. But, if you haven't found a desirable marriage partner when you are in your mid-twenties, I'd certainly advise you to have an affair, because I would not want you to miss out on this very wonderful dimension of life. And if you're ever in any kind of difficulty — remember — you can always come home." Pretty progressive and reassuring advice for a father to give to his daughter sixty years ago! Mother would cluck and admit that when she was a girl, she could never have gotten answers to the specific kind of questions I was asking my Dad.

Although Al's parents had been more traditional and conservative than mine, he came into wedlock with lots more swinging experience. He had chased a series of girls up and down the Santa Monica Canyon in hopped-up cars while I was still a good little German school girl. He had lost one wife and divorced another, and we were both determined to make this marriage work. Yet, when I think back now, our premarital discussions seem surprisingly simplistic and naive. We certainly didn't have the vaguest premonition of what Gail Sheehy, author of *Passages,* calls "predictable crises of adult life!" We learned by trial and error.

My two years of military experience in the Coast Guard during World War II had certainly broadened my outlook on sex. There I found my own position marked just one spot on a social continuum. Some of the young women for whom I was responsible were a lot more conservative than I, while others were more enterprising in their activities. I learned to like and respect one girl who was striking it rich, entertaining sailors in her apartment in town during off-duty hours. She was one of my best and most reliable workers. I could always count on Kelly to be on time and efficient. Long after our discharge, when I was back in a New York office working from nine to five, she was still sending me glorious full-color postcards from Hawaii saying "wish you were here!" For the first time I encountered women who were Lesbians. I was also involved in counseling with one SPAR who had resorted to an illegal abortion while another single woman would not think of having her pregnancy terminated. (In the service both homosexuality and illegal abortions were punishable offenses in military courts.) I began to realize that my own position on sexual matters was as uniquely mine as my fingerprints.

My substitute teaching in the Fort Bragg schools in the early fifties contributed to our ability as a family to become more open about "birds and bees" issues.

Several times I happened into the high school all girls' class in "family life education" — sex education of sorts. Invariably the students asked, "Why are they teaching us this stuff now? We needed it in fifth or sixth grade."

Occasionally I bumbled into boys' biology just as their textbook discussed female menstruation. Perfect opening for giggles and snickers and I had no advance warning, but decided there was no cause for panic. After all these were just nice little boys like the one I had at home (which ain't necessarily so, because junior high school kids tend to be brats when they have a substitute). So I waded right into the subject on the assumption they all had mothers or sisters at home and would be having girl friends, wives, daughters — and questions in due time. I introduced the topic by explaining that menstruation is a natural process, that there are many different scientific and slang words for it, and that they had better stop being silly and learn about it. It went okay. I became increasingly able to talk about matters of sexual functioning in a relaxed manner and that was a great step forward.

Back home at the kitchen table Al's and my first arguments about our approach to the children's sexuality began when they were still quite small. Al had an earthy, corny sense of humor which was quite irrepressible. He loved puns and limericks, and the mere hint of anything sexual brought out the best (or worst) in him. He would spontaneously burst out with jokes . "Al. Please. Not in front of the children," I'd protest. He could not understand that I wanted to keep the subject innocent and ideal for them. I took sex seriously and had to learn about its lighthearted aspects under his tutelage.

Trying to stay one step ahead of our children in their social/sexual learning process accustomed us to sudden, startling questions. They rarely waited for an appropriate time or place. There was seldom time for us to prepare ourselves. They wanted to know now, and if the answer was too long-winded, they might go on to something else. Sometimes they weren't ready for technical details and would ask the same question again later. One friend of mine settled down to give her young adolescent son a well thought out, serious explanation of intercourse and was totally undone because he laughed merrily. She never did find out what struck him funny. She was so upset that she vowed to make her husband take his turn with their other boys.

Basically, both Al and I tried to help our children understand that the subject of sex is not a secret, but that it *is* a private and personal part of their lives. Barbara needed specific, repeated explanations of certain ground rules which David and Karen had picked up on their own. Not long after she had wondered about the fat man's belly, we were downtown on a fine sunny day. A convertible zipped by with the top down, and the guy driving it was bare chested. "Ooh!" yelled Barbara. "He's all naked."

"No, he's not," I said "He only took his shirt off."

"It's okay for boys to take their tops off," added David anxiously.

"So you see, Barbara," I continued, "he's not naked because he is a boy and he only took his shirt off." And with that I caught my young son's eye and we both burst out laughing. We had heard the inanity of our dialogue, and yet it was important for Barbara to learn this particular nuance of where one can do what and when.

Lucky that she was the youngest of three, so Al and I had an idea of what to expect in children's behavior, and Karen and David automatically helped with the process of educating their sister. "No, Barbara! You can't come out like that. Put your nightgown on!" one of them would yell as she toddled out into the living room naked, and they'd wheel her around and push her back into the bedroom. Or they'd shout at her to close the bathroom door behind her. Such small object lessons in appropriate social behavior have to precede more advanced knowledge in sexual mores and morals. In spite of this, she often embarrassed me when she was a little girl. She'd walk up behind unsuspecting gentlemen who were peacefully reading their paper in the library, and give them big hugs. I could not explain to them that this pretty little girl felt warmly towards the world and had not yet learned to channel these feelings appropriately.

When we were in Denmark Barbara, at seventeen, really learned to test her "independence wings." One day she and I were riding a streetcar and landed in separate seats with Barbara a few rows in front of me. There was clearly something about her robust rosy appearance that seemed to appeal to Danish men. I had noticed this before, so I wasn't too surprised to see a young man sit down beside her. He began to talk to her — first in Danish, then English. He came on strong, obviously trying to pick her up, and at first Barbara looked pleased. But when he tried to put his arm around her, she became uncomfortable and glanced back to me as if she expected me to intercede. Finally, just as we were getting to our stop, she pointed to me and shouted in his ear, "That's my Mom, Lotte!"

It was our Danish experience of 1971 that really started the wheels turning in my head. The Danes have a realistic, relaxed attitude towards relationships between men and women, those with mental retardation naturally included. While Barbara spent the month living in the Copenhagen group home, it was still a residence for young women only, but boyfriends were very much a part of the everyday scenery.

Discussions of each resident's problems with relationships, dating, birth control, marriage and child rearing were tackled individually as they came up. Either Elna Skov, the director, or one of her well-trained care assistants would sit down with the young woman, and sometimes her boyfriend, and they would discuss matters of physiology and contraception. There were no specially prepared textbooks then. Elna used an old book of home nursing advice, which was richly illustrated, and began her instruction with what we would now call "their baseline," wherever the individual happened to be. "The majority of our young women don't know much when they come here from the institution or from their own families. So I try to find out what they know and what puzzles them, and go from there. And when they tell me, 'My boyfriend is afraid to use a condom,' for whatever reason, then I know that it's time to invite him to sit in on our lessons."

Barbara really didn't live in the group home long enough to become involved in dating activities, and without an outside work assignment she had little opportunity to meet young men. Surprisingly the language barrier turned out not to be much of a barrier at all, and the reason may have been that Barbara had become used to communicating across her own speech handicap. At any rate she managed well. She felt free to visit the other young women in their rooms and worked along happily in the kitchen with the housekeeper who didn't speak a word of English.

On her evaluation report the staff persons noted: "Barbara gets along well with peers and friends — does not seem to need more social contact — but wants sexual contact badly."

I came home with my mother's heart in a state of palpitation. Conflicting thoughts and feelings tossed and turned, especially in the area of sexuality. I was trying to sort out what I had learned and come to grips with my parental fears for Barbara. I needed to examine my own ambivalent attitudes on such loaded issues as masturbation, premarital sex, birth control, homosexuality, and abortion.

I was certainly not alone in my quest for answers. Others were reaching the same point of concern. I found out about a workshop on the subject of sexuality, organized by a pediatrician. She had invited a special education teacher with some of his students, and me, as a parent, to take part in the discussion.

First thing in the morning the good doctor drew some charts and graphs on the blackboard to illustrate the incidence of mental retardation in children born to mothers with the same disability. It was high compared with national norms. It struck me as a discouraging beginning, unsubstantiated as it was by comparable figures of mothers who, though developmentally delayed, might have passed into the so-called normal population. I felt scared rather than reassured, and I was reminded that much of our then current knowledge of "mental retardation" was still rooted in the eugenics movement of the early twentieth century which had frightened the public into believing that those with the labels of idiots and imbeciles would outbreed us all.

The students, thank goodness, did not join us until later in the day. They were a bunch of giggly teenage boys and girls who nervously attempted to field personal questions about their social needs and desires, thrown at them by a group of total strangers. They all attended a school in a rural area, and most of them lived on ranches and helped with the care of animals and other farm chores. One pretty girl with Down Syndrome was able to express some of her frustration at having to go everywhere with her mom and dad while her brothers and sisters took off on their own because they could drive. The students appeared totally unaware of their adolescent feelings and relationships.

After they left the room the discussion ranged widely. Someone made the point that they might remain innocently childlike and continue to be sexually unaware. This was challenged by a group home staff person who thought that there *was* need for social training and instruction in sexuality. One father anxiously and repeatedly protested, "Our Jim has never even thought about sex or gone near a girl.

He kisses his mother goodnight — that's all. Leave him alone! You'll only stir him up."

I couldn't believe that it was worse to "stir up" feelings of closeness and affection that are real, than to bury them by evasion. I thought of the many clues and signals that our children had given of their social and sexual maturing.

There had been a puzzling situation when Karen told us that she and the little boy who came to play with her (I seem to remember that they were both about kindergarten age) had a good time "playing house" in a secluded spot in our garden. She went on to say that he liked to "play doctor," which she graphically explained as his wanting to examine her genital area. Both Al and I were good friends with his parents but we felt uncomfortable and didn't know how to handle the situation. Was it just normal curiosity, or was he somehow coercing her into an activity that made her feel uncomfortable also? And how to discourage it without making her feel guilty? I believe I did mention it to his Mom and we decided to steer their play into other directions. The family moved away — somewhat to my relief.

All three of our children routinely bounced into our bed to snuggle on Sunday mornings. Imperceptibly this tapered off during Karen's and David's adolescence. If we thought about it at all, we must have assumed that they were establishing contact with someone of the opposite sex, at least in their imagination. But what about Barbara? What was she to do with her need for warmth and touching? What would take the place of snuggling in bed with her parents when this no longer seemed appropriate or possible?

We noticed that she was masturbating. She'd sit in a comfortable armchair in the living room, rub her thighs together and jiggle with pleasure. By then we had learned that masturbation was not harmful, contrary to the messages of our own childhood. Even in a family as medically sophisticated as mine, there seemed to have been reluctance to permit children to stimulate their bodies. I vaguely recalled a bedtime scene when Papi brought Aunt Martha, his sister who was a pediatrician, to my bedroom to tuck me in. I was almost asleep, snuggled under the covers, when they lowered their voices to a whisper. With my rabbit ears I thought I heard something about not letting me keep my hands under the covers. Even though I wasn't quite sure what I heard, I pulled my arms out to give them both hugs. I wondered about it later and learned to keep my masturbating activities strictly private.

In Barbara's case we said repeatedly and firmly, "Not here. Not in the living room, Barbara. We know it feels good to jiggle, but it belongs in the privacy of your bedroom or bathroom. You must learn this too."

David was an adult when he admitted he'd had unanswered question about masturbation when he was a kid. "I never saw you do it," I said in surprise, "and Dad and I simply assumed that you knew it was okay, Son."

"Yeah," he said, "but I got plenty of conflicting messages from the community. It would have helped if you'd brought up the subject. Remember the time Sam and I went camping? How'd ya think we got poison oak on our genitals?"

The fact that old wives' tales about masturbation still abound in this day and age is scarily real. It came clear to me a few years ago when I was invited to talk to a parent group about social and family life education for their adult sons and daughters. I took along a British film, *Like Other People,* in which young people with cerebral palsy who lived in a residence, touchingly and eloquently discussed their feelings about relationships and love.

It was a group of elderly parents in a small, conservative logging and fishing community who found it difficult to talk about such personal subjects, so there were no immediate comments when I turned off the projector. A young man in the back of the room liked the film very much. The feelings expressed were "right on." I was glad he got the discussion rolling.

When the meeting broke up he came to the front and said hesitantly, "There was something I wanted to ask but I didn't want to ask in front of the others. Is it true that masturbating can cause brain damage? That's what my mother told me. She says that's the cause of my being slow."

"No!" I said, "But there are many others of our generation who were told the same thing by their mothers and fathers." He smiled and thanked me. Then he turned back to the young woman who was standing next to him. He put his hand lightly on her shoulder and said, "Of course, now that I have a woman I don't need it anymore."

He understood love, as did one of the young men in the film who, when asked, "Can retarded people love?" answered,

> "Being retarded has nothing to do with love. They're capable of very deep love. Those who are intellectually able have more interests — more ways to substitute for love. If you're retarded you give your whole being to love."

Barbara matured physically earlier than either Karen or I. She was only eleven when she yelled to me from the bathroom one day: "Mummy, Mummy, come quick!" When I rushed to see what had happened, she was beaming. "Look! I got my period." She was probably not able to understand all the intricacies of female plumbing which caused the flow of blood, but she knew that it happened every month and that we bathed routinely and wore a pad or tampon. Karen and I had made it a point to tell her about our menstrual periods and to show her matter-of-factly how we took care of them. Barbara was looking forward to the event as a status symbol of adulthood. Unfortunately, it turned out to be a false alarm. She had eaten a lot of fresh beets the night before!

When Barbara actually did have her first period some time later, it was a terrible disappointment. Not only did it hurt, but it went on for days — almost two weeks. We finally had to consult our doctor, who prescribed small doses of birth control pills which regulated matters. She still grouches occasionally, but has learned to accept menstrual periods as a respected part of the female condition.

Barbara established her right to privacy on the day after Bob Perske had spoken at our first major California conference on the sexuality of our children. He told us of his swing around the Scandinavian countries and brought great news of educational and living arrangements for persons with developmental special needs. He discussed privacy in the Danish group homes that he had visited. Barbara was at the conference with us, but I didn't think that she had paid attention to much that was being discussed. The next day I went barreling into our bathroom while she was sitting on the toilet, and she yelled out, "Stop! Knock first!" I reeled back with a red face, knocked, re-entered, and said, "Hey, you heard what Mr. Perske said yesterday, didn't you?" She smiled and nodded.

And remember the automatic prohibition against sex that I had vowed to uphold? Well I had to reverse that when she was quite a young teenager. A student from our activity center was spending the weekend at our house while his parents were away. One day I saw the two of them sitting on the sofa hand in hand. He seemed a bit embarrassed, but Barbara beamed at him adoringly. Right then I knew that we could not possibly relegate all boy/girl relationships into never-never land for her. It would be cruel to keep this essential dimension of life from her.

We were lucky to have had Karen and David first, for they readied us for the funny misunderstandings and confusions of all children as they ask and learn about sex. Barbara found it more difficult to ask questions, but we learned to listen for cues. I could see question marks in her eyes and sense situations that were going to be puzzling for her. And the rural environment helped — or so we thought.

One evening when Al came home he looked out the window to the field across the road and announced: "Hey, Mr. Gregg's horse got married, I hear, and soon she's going to have a baby." Sure enough five-year old Karen asked how horses get married, and Al threw me a despairing glance.

I answered for him. "Well, children, Mr. Gregg took the mummy horse down the road to Mr. Junker who has a daddy horse, and the daddy horse put the seed inside the mummy horse's tummy, so now the baby is growing inside the mummy, and will soon come out. Horses are different from people though. They don't live in families like we do, so the mummy and the baby may not see the daddy very often."

Karen continued to look puzzled and said," I don't understand, Mom. Horses don't dance, do they?"

It was my turn to be puzzled. "What do you mean, dear?"

"Well," said Karen, "I don't see how horses can marry if they can't dance at their wedding."

The biology had obviously been wasted on her, but there was a sequel to the story. The foal was born and was galloping around the field about a year and a half later when David was about five. As I was keeping him company while he waited for the school bus one day, he wanted to know if the foal had come out of the mummy horse's tummy and how did it get there? I gave him verbatim the same answer as I had given to Karen, but when I mentioned Mr. Junker, David interrupted, "Mr. Junker? Why him? Why didn't Mr. Gregg take her to Mr. Windus?" Mr. Windus happened to be his best buddy's father and they didn't own a horse, so I was stumped again.

"The Winduses don't have a horse, do they David?"

"Oh," said David thoughtfully, "it has to be another horse."

We accumulated and nurtured a variety of pets over the years. Besides a number of country cats, there was always one dog. At one point Karen won a duck at a carnival tossing a dime into a dish. Peeper grew up to be a mean beast who terrorized our favorite cat. Then there was a large turtle. Al drilled a hole through its shell so that Karen could take it for walks on a leash. We also raised a couple of lambs whose mothers were unable to take good care of twins, or "bummers" as they were called by the ranchers. Each time a lamb was ready to return to the ranch, their owner wanted to repay us with a leg of lamb, and that presented a distinct problem. We couldn't possibly *eat* "Ora" or "Ditto." We surreptitiously hid the gift in the freezer.

Karen and David saw to it that Barbara took her turn with the responsibilities of caring for these pets as soon as she was able. Only Chips, Karen's mare, was too large for her to handle. She did sit on her and walked around the yard, and shared with Karen her minor triumphs of horsemanship at the riding club rodeo.

Dogs continued to be our main pets, and we preferred boy dogs. Al thought we were too busy for the additional work of raising puppies and we turned down several offers of cute female dogs who happened to need a good home. Well, one time we were had. A shaggy little mutt showed up on our doorstep to visit and to eat. He/she looked like nothing much and wouldn't stand still for closer inspection. Our neighbors assured us that it was a male and had been deliberately dropped off from a passing car. The children named it Prince and begged us to keep it, but Al and I refused. It would have to be a trip to the pound.

Just then Karen appeared with Barbara in tow. "You can't give that dog away, now, Dad. It's 'Princess,' not 'Prince.' She and George just got married. Barbara and I saw it."

So Princess stayed and became one of ours. When she went into labor, there was tremendous excitement and Al even came home from work for the event. She gave birth right under the kitchen window and Barbara could see each of the five little sacks as they came out and were licked clean into wiggly little pups.

It was real life education, at a time when most of our children with developmental special needs were still woefully insulated from real information. Most of them had trouble asking questions and the words in books remained a blank. Rarely were they able to look at sexually explicit materials like other children, and TV has always been more erotically stimulating than informative. Until quite recently special education classes steered away from family life education for our sons and daughters. They had to grow up and tell us of their own needs.

When I first worked as a counselor at the summer camp for young adults back in 1960, we were told in our counselor indoctrination, "Now this is a bit like a resort, and there may be some infatuations. If you see a boy and girl walking down the trail with their arms around each other or holding hands, we suggest that you just walk between them, put your arms on their shoulders, and say something like, 'hey, isn't it a nice day!'"

That was totally simplistic and superficial advice, and no solution for our fears for Barbara at a time when she was entering adolescence. There came a day when we heard of a young woman in a nearby town's sheltered workshop who had become pregnant. We were told that she was poorly supervised at home and had a history of acting out sexually. She was socially less responsible than Barbara but we became frightened. We panicked. We could not seem to square our new-found awareness of Barbara's need for warmth and friendship with our concern for her safety and well-being. We sought advice from a physician and arranged for her to have a tubal ligation. Barbara trusted this doctor, and she trusted us. We all hid behind his advice to her that she needed to have her appendix taken out, and she and I did not talk about the primary purpose of the surgery until much, much later. Even so, as the day of the surgery came closer, Al and I felt the weight of our action. We were aware that we were manipulating a human being. Now I know that we should have waited. Barbara should have been a partner in this decision which affected one of the basic functions of her body. She understood much more than we gave her credit for, and later she was able to express to me her sense of loss and deprivation. Later I also found out about the abominable situation that existed in many state institutions across the country where young women — without their permission or knowledge — underwent this surgical procedure as a prerequisite for returning to life in the community.

I did not think then, and do not think now, that Barbara could be responsible for the care of a child. Thus a tubal ligation was still the simplest and best way for our daughter, but it should and could have waited until she was older and we could have discussed it with her honestly.

A poignant letter "To Kirsten," from a Danish mother, which my mentor, Rosemary Dybwad, translated, profoundly moved me. It was written on the eve of her own daughter's sterilization operation. She says that her girl is nineteen, pretty, and well able to take care of her daily living needs, but she is physically handicapped by cerebral palsy and the physicians advise that childbirth would be too risky. It is an agonizing letter which concludes as follows:

> I, your mother, have explained to you all the disadvantages of a pregnancy, have told you about the heavy responsibility of bringing a child into the world, told you what a burden it would be for your health, for your future, for your independence — and I have done this based on what I believe

and believe very deeply and after many struggles — is best for you. And at the same time I feel guilty.

There has been a lot of consultation. All kinds of papers have gone back and forth. Some people have talked with you and some with both of us — and tomorrow — you will be the same girl, lively and dear, but without the ability to have a child.

That will be tomorrow — another day — another Kirsten. I wonder if I took time enough, words enough to tell you about the joys of being a mother.

I feel with this mother more deeply than I can say.

It was not until several years later that Barbara first spoke of the tubal ligation. She was having her period and complaining about cramps. I was suggesting that she take a Midol when she burst out, "Why didn't you take it all out?"

I was astounded. She had obviously found out about the consequences of the operation while I hadn't the guts to talk to her about it. She must have also heard from other young women, who had both their ovaries and uterus removed, that this eliminated having periods.

I spoke with Barbara as frankly as I was able. I told her why we thought that she would be better off not having babies, but that I'm truly sorry we did not tell her about it before the operation. I tried to assure her that it's okay to be a woman without a baby, like her Aunt Grace, her sister Karen and many others. I can't remember exactly what she said because the pain of it all has blurred my memory, but I know she somehow conveyed to me she felt cheated and sad. Occasionally the subject has come up again. And she loves babies.

In some ways Barbara benefited by her brother's and sister's late blooming adolescence, and it gave us all time to catch up with one another's changing attitudes. For many years I was more concerned about the social progress of our two older ones than about their sexual precocity. They were both comparatively short and chubby — definitely not "in" with the popular kids — and while Karen agonized about her lack of popularity I was secretly relieved that I did not yet have to face the heavy responsibility of coping with a sexually active teenager. We had it easy compared to the parents of today.

It was not until Karen and David returned from college with their friends and openly challenged our ground rules about boys sleeping in the boys' room and girls in the girls' room that we began to have differences of opinion. Al and I argued bitterly with them about the appropriateness of these sleeping arrangements under our roof and about respect for our values. They called us uptight and hypocritical. Karen won the last round in these debates. "Do you want to know me as I really am, Mother?" she challenged one day, "or shall I lie?" With that began a more mature, adult relationship, in which we were able to respect and accept each other's differing values.

We found their honesty admirable. Their accusation of hypocrisy hit home. We needed some of this same gutsiness with which they stood up to us in order to defend Barbara's right to be a sexual human being. We also needed it to shore up our own worries as she ventured forth into their free-wheeling world.

For Barbara and her peers privacy was and still is hard to come by. Too many of them ride back and forth in their little bus or van from their own home or group home to the day's activity, stealthily holding hands. Even at parties for holidays and other special occasions they have about as much privacy as peas in a pod. Then, when they reach the magic age of legal adulthood, we expect them to somehow accomplish responsible adult behavior.

There was one memorable small occasion when Barbara experienced a moment of essential human warmth. She was home when good friends and their three daughters came to visit for the weekend. They brought along the mother's teenage brother, who has Down Syndrome. All beds were taken, and Stanley rolled out his brand-new sleeping bag on the living room rug and slept soundly. The next evening Barbara dragged out her sleeping bag and announced that she would sleep in the living room with Stanley and did. After our friends had left, she confided to me with a radiant smile that she and Stanley had kissed before they went to sleep.

It was during those early Paul Bunyan School days of the sixties that my partner Dodie and I decided it was time to add some factual information about our bodies to the curriculum, and launched into a lesson on menstruation. All we had as a teaching aid were some free, well illustrated booklets from a sanitary napkin company. When I phoned Dodie to check on the results of this monumental lesson, she reported, "Not much happened. It was sorta disappointing. I think they were more interested in the circus that's coming to town." We re-signed ourselves to trying another time. Barbara came home that day brandishing some free circus tickets, and that's all we talked about at first. Later that evening I thought I heard her say something about eggs to her Dad. I wasn't sure I had heard right. "Dodie teach about eggs," she said, "today — in school — my eggs down here," and pat-ted herself on the lower abdomen. So something had landed after all! Not much, but it was a beginning.

Her understanding has become more sophisticated now. During her nurse practitioner training, Karen decided to teach a short family life education class to Barbara and some of her friends. By then the teaching aids had developed into plastic models of the lower half of both men's and women's bodies with parts that they could not only see and touch, but remove and replace. Karen told me the class went well, and it reinforced my belief that such access to information and to presentations and discussions interested Barbara in a factual way. It was a needed component of "growing up" for her and her peers just as for all young people.

A more mature and experienced Barbara (now 41) gave me a great opportunity for woman-to-woman talk when she was home one eve-ning last year. She was flipping through the *New Yorker,* stopped and handed it to me. "Look, Lotte! I like this." She pointed to a smallish ad for a copy of a sculpture of Hercules and Diomedes — both of them naked, Hercules lifting Diomedes who is holding on to his pe-nis. "Can I buy this?" Barbara asked.

I explained that it cost $498. "What do you want to do with it?"

"Give it to Fred," she said matter-of-factly.

"I have a postcard of this in my file," I told her. "Would you like a copy?" (Many years ago good friends had sent it to us from Florence and Al and I had wondered what our mailman thought of it. I had filed it under sexuality.)

A few minutes later Barbara spoke again, seriously. "Lotte, what is love?" That led to quite a conversation about different kinds of love for different people, like for Karen and David and me and of course for Fred. I asked how she feels when she loves different people. Does she want to touch? Do things for them? Help them? Give presents? Have sex? Go out together? At that point she brought up marriage again.

She seemed quite clear about the differences, and it was the labors of Hercules and the penis that brought up her question and some of the answers. What a teaching aid that long-ago card from Florence had become.

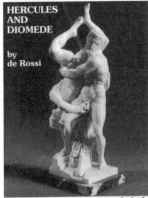

HERCULES AND DIOMEDE by de Rossi

Hercules—the enduring symbol of heroism. This dramatic 16th century statue depicts one of the hero's twelve mythological labors. The original is in the Palazzo Vecchio, Florence, Italy. Bonded marble reproduction is 20" high on marble base...$498 ppd. Check, VISA, MC. Unqualified guarantee.

Barbara and Fred at Blue Grass Festival, 1984

*Fred grieving for his two mothers who died and for one of his childhood
friends who also died. They are depicted in this colored pencil drawing,
which was later made into a T-shirt by the Cypress Street Center.*

Chapter 12

Love, Death and Other Realities

We tend to shield our sons and daughters, especially those with disabilities, from the inevitability of the end of life. Death has touched Barbara's life several times over the years. We have lost grandparents, a close young friend, and good neighbors. Beloved dogs and cats met with sudden accidents. Again and again Barbara asked, "Where is Nana now? What is Jack doing?" We have tried to lead her towards accepting the fact that death comes to us all and that it will come to her too. "We all die, Barb," I'd say. "Every day there are babies born all over the world, and old people die." "Not me. I'm not going to," and with that she would shake her head and turn off the conversation.

Death came home to Barbara and to all of us in 1981. It began on an ordinary Sunday. We all knew Al was fighting angina pains and was — in his own words — trying to do everything right for his heart since experiencing his second heart attack. He was no longer smoking his pipe, he'd cut way down on coffee, and he was taking part in a cardiac rehab exercise program sponsored by the Mendocino Coast District Hospital. He was proud of his growing endurance, and we were proud of him. When his doctor gave occasional lectures to the group and invited the spouses, I attended, listened, and learned. Karen, who had worked in a hospital coronary intensive care unit, watched worriedly from afar.

I too worried, because there were two things Al would not give up.

He loved to go to the beach on a rare sunny Sunday and dunk in the frigid ocean, and I *knew* that this might fibrillate the heart. And he continued valiantly to saw and cut wood. Not with a chain saw. He spurned that and preferred his trusty handsaw. I'd watch from the house and when I saw him take a break I suspected he might be having a chest pain. I tried not to bug him with questions. "I'm lucky," he would say. "I always get a small warning sensation and Dr. H. says it's okay to do this as long as I take it slow and easy. So I stop and rest a few moments and it goes away." Soon he'd be back at work. I don't remember his ever reaching for the nitroglycerin pills he was supposed to keep in his shirt pocket!

And then it hit. Al had returned to the house and settled into his favorite recliner. I was typing in the adjoining room when he called me, "I think I'm having a heart attack." And he was, and we both knew.

His two weeks in our hospital were full of dramatic ups and downs. There was fear, anxiety, and loving care from our family, the staff of the hospital and the coastal community. There were also moments of laughter. And when Barbara drove up with her sister she became a full participant with us. Al was restless and uncomfortable for the first few days. Several times he asked, "*Why* did this happen? I thought I was doing everything right." Then one afternoon when Barbara, Karen and I were with him, he seemed to be a bit more alert and cheerful and asked me to raise his bed. When I did, and looked up, his eyes seemed to roll back into their sockets and he passed out.

Karen saw it instantly and shouted, "Roll down the bed! Cardiac arrest!" and she pushed the Code Blue button and leaned over her father to begin CPR. The staff rushed in and pushed the three of us out of the room and we huddled at the nurses' station holding each other's hands tightly — frightened to death.

A few endless moments later a nurse stuck her head out from the ICU and said Al was going to be okay. That's when Barbara let go of my hand, heaved a deep sigh and asked, "Why did you ever marry him, Mummy?" I was speechless. But then it flashed through my head that she was reacting to the pain — her father's and ours — and how she wished all of this wasn't happening. A doctor whom we knew was working on his charts on the other side of the desk. He heard Barbara's question and before I could recover my voice, "Why, Barbara," he said, "if your Mom hadn't married Al there would have been no you. She married him so she could have Karen and David and you." And that was just right and seemed to satisfy her for the moment. I have always been grateful to him.

The intensity of the next few days was unbelievably difficult to bear, but when David and his wife Judy showed up, things brightened. We had been unable to find them on their camping trip in Canada and they just happened to come by on their way south. It gave Al joy to find out Judy was going to have our first grandchild and that they would be moving from Los Angeles to Seattle. Barbara was living near Karen, who was starting a challenging new job in San Francisco and thought that she and Barbara would soon be able to return to their work and routine for a while. We all felt just a little better.

All along the doctors were wonderful about consulting with each other and with heart specialists in San Francisco. They spent endless hours watching and worrying and reported to us the changing conditions and treatment. Karen had recently become a nurse practitioner. The doctors made her feel like a member of their team.

Al had lots of visitors. I took one couple to Cap'n Flints, a local fish restaurant, where the ladies room has a "Poop Deck News" chalk board. Somebody had written on it, "Al Moise is better!" I told him and it made him smile.

Barbara heard many of these discussions and sensed and shared our deep fears. One time she asked abruptly, "Is Al going to die, Mom?" So Karen and I tried to explain to her how mixed up our own feelings were. How on the one hand — when things were going a little better — we had hopes Al would get all well again. Yet there was the danger something awful might happen — like another cardiac arrest — and that then he might die. "It feels like knots of fear and flutters of hope all mixed up inside," I told her. "It feels terrible," Karen said. Barbara nodded understandingly.

Al did improve, and when his pacemaker had settled down he was allowed to leave ICU for a regular room. The children returned to their own routines. One day I tried to ask Al if he was frightened, but he glossed over my questions and said he wasn't scared. "Our doctors are the best," he said, but he did mention the good old Eskimo custom of taking old folks out on the ice to die. "That's what I wish you could do for me. I can't bear to think of becoming frail and feeble." We didn't talk about it often. When Al began to talk about going home I asked the doctor what he might be able to do. He said that much would depend on how much damage his heart muscle had sustained and we'd have to wait and see. When Al admitted to Karen (with whom he talked on the phone every day) that he was still awfully weak and tired, she cautioned him to be patient and that this time the recovery might take longer. "I know," he said, "but your mother is good at that sort of thing."

He died quietly and suddenly on the third Sunday. His heart just stopped, and the autopsy did show severe damage to the heart muscle. He would have had to lead the restricted life he abhorred. For us his death came too early. For Al it was right.

When Barbara and Karen drove back to Fort Bragg together Karen said that she could not understand what was happening to Barbara. "All the way up I've been weeping and asking her to hand me Kleenex, and she is as bright and cheerful as can be. It worries me. Her affect is all wrong."

I turned to Barbara and put my arms around her and asked, "What's the matter? It's okay to be sad and to cry when someone dies."

"I try to be brave," she said, "but it hurts to cry!" and then I could see the tears in her eyes. She seemed unable to admit her father was dead and tried to hide behind a bright and brave front.

So Karen and I decided to ask the funeral director if it was possible for Barbara to see her father. He understood, and said she could come the next morning. Karen and Barbara went to the funeral parlor together. She seemed totally unafraid. "He looks like he's still alive," she said as she cradled his head and kissed him, then turned to Karen and observed, "he feels like clay." Then she tried to pull back the sheet that covered him, but the funeral director moved fast and stopped her. When she came home she seemed sadly content.

We all gathered for a memorial celebration in a church in Mendocino. Hundreds came and spoke. We laughed and cried and there was music. It was a great gathering. Perhaps not quite the wake Al had requested, but close to it. Our family and countless friends shored each other up for a life without him. Al would have been pleased and proud.

Barbara and I talk of Al often and of our grandparents and others whom we have loved. When she is sad I try to remind her of the many happy times we had together. I ask her if she can "call up" their faces — remember what their voices sounded like. Just a few weeks ago — out of the clear blue sky — she interrupted her dishwashing, turned around to me and asked, "When you go to heaven, Lotte, who do you want to see?"

Taken aback, I countered with another question, "Who do *you* want to see, Barbara?"

"Al?" she said with a question mark.

"Yes, Al!" I said, and that was the end of the conversation.

She has taken a small step towards acknowledging death as an inevitable part of the human condition, but the thought still pains her. "What is going to happen to me when you die?" she exploded one day when she was home for the weekend. "And who's going to live in our house?" She had never said "when" before, and never had she brought up the question of the house in which we had lived ever since she can remember. "I don't know, Barbara," is not an answer that she accepts easily, but it seems to me that with her "when" question she has established a first wobbly bridgehead to that scary future place.

We have continued to try to help her with the loss of anchor persons in her life by facing her grief squarely. I learned my own lesson from a conversation I overheard in a group home for adults. One of the residents had just found out that her elderly father had died. A new staff person asked the resident nurse for advice on the situation. "Why don't you give her a tranquilizer," I heard her say, and was appalled. What a repressive, unfeeling way of coping with pain. What a blatant denial of that young woman's humanness to buffer her grief with a pill!

We all have encouraged Barbara to remember and talk about the people who are gone, and whom we loved and always will. Although we celebrate most traditional holidays, we have never been a formally religious family. Heaven, hell, and resurrection are concepts that are difficult to explain, but she has heard about them when she goes to church, and she likes to go to church. She has also witnessed funeral services where ashes were strewn over the ocean.

"And then the memories of the person who is dead live in our minds — in our head," I have said. "I remember my parents way back when I was a little girl, Barbara. Some memories are sad, but mostly I remember happy things about them. I can still see their faces and hear their voices in my memory. That's the way it's going to be for you too, I hope. And you will have your brother and sister and many, many friends to be close to you and care about you."

We have held this dialogue not once but several times. It hurts both of us each time, like growing pains, and she will continue to ask out loud as long as she questions death in her heart.

Sometimes the conversation takes an unexpected turn as when we were having breakfast with our close friend, Linda, who is a social worker counselor working in the San Francisco school district. "Why don't you be my mother, Linda, when she dies?" Barbara asked her, pointing in my direction.

"I can't be your mother," Linda answered honestly, "but I can be your friend and I want to be."

"And Karen and David will be your guardians," I began, but Barbara interrupted me in mid-sentence. "Why don't you do it and get it over with!" she blurted out and left Linda and me speechless.

The reality and sadness of death and dying seem to continue to be in Barbara's consciousness, but she has added another dimention to her repertoire of feelings, and that is love beyond her immediate family. Fred came into her life when she first went to the group home in Cotati — the home to which her Regional Center counselor had introduced her.

Fred is a few years younger than Barbara. His father was in the military and stationed in Newfoundland where Fred was born (a fact that impresses me more than it does him). He has Down Syndrome with some of the recognizable facial characteristics. He is lucky to be strong, healthy and capable. His short stature and poor speech have in no way stood in the way of his and Barbara's growing friendship.

Fred's parents lived in Fort Bragg when I met them briefly while Fred attended our school, and then his mother died. I don't know how soon after her death Fred moved to Cotati, but I do know that he still mourns the death of his mom deeply. He has never been able to describe to me the sequence of happenings of his life during that time.

Fred and Barbara became friends gradually. They traveled home together on weekend visits — Fred to his Dad's, who had remarried, in Fort Bragg, and Barbara to our home. They also began to spend time together at Karen's house. There they had privacy and opportunity to become more "snuggly." It was a luxury that the group home did not afford. At Karen's they rolled out their sleeping bags on the living room floor and Karen could hear them have long conversations before they went to sleep. Their relationship was surely strengthened by these lengthy pillow talks.

All seemed to be going along well for our family. David and Judy with their children, Leah and Jacob, were happy with working and playing in Seattle. They seemed far away but not distant. Barbara was happy to have her sister so close, and the Greyhound Bus was still running up to Fort Bragg. I continued to be busier than a bird dog running around the State of California and the world. Most of my activities centered on advocacy for persons with special needs and my ongoing battles with the bureaucracy of developmental services in California.

1983 turned into what I think of as Barbara's "betrayal." I had a major adventure, which took me to Nepal half way up Everest with a small trekking group. Two of the group were friends from the Mendocino Coast, and together the three of us were a hundred ninety nine years old! I had always been a mountain lover. The Himalayas were the fulfillment of a dream, and there too — in Kathmandu for a week by myself before our trekking group assembled — I was able to connect with a small school where I could comfortably help work with children with special needs. I also discovered that one of our Sherpa guides had a daughter with cerebral palsy. He invited me to his home to meet his wife and two little girls, and we became friends and have remained friends across continents and cultures.

When I came home I hit bottom — literally and hard. Down from fourteen thousand feet to sea level I was met by reality. I found that program cuts had come down from the Department of Developmental Services and affected Barbara's home-away-from-home. She would no longer be able to stay at Penngrove House where she had been receiving specialized services to further develop her skills. I felt totally out of control over my daughter's life and watched with fear in my heart as our system kept Barbara hopelessly unsettled and homeless for most of that year.

She had been living in that house so harmoniously — close to her sister — able to come home by Greyhound. She had learned new skills, made real friends, and considered Sonoma County her other home. Then, for most of the year 1984 she literally lived out of a suitcase.

She moved twice that summer. The first house had an independent living skills program which was designed to move persons into apartment living. It was too demanding for Barbara. The next home placement met a snag when the manager found she could not outwait the Regional Center's reimbursement process for Barbara. There was a third attempt to place her in a home which she liked on her trial visit, but this also got hung up in a bureaucratic rule devised by the Regional Center Board of Directors.

Barbara internalized all of this. She felt unwanted. Her performance at her work center plummeted and I heard her say, "They want me out of here, Mom!" — or, as she picked up on discussions of rates and reimbursement: "They want more money for me."

Her sister and I stood by with heavy hearts, and finally went through an unpleasant process called a "Fair Hearing." Fair Hearings are frequently standard operating procedures for service providing agencies. They are designed to protect both the parents and their off-spring, but their scenario is somewhat threatening and causes parents to be afraid. On a previous occasion I had voiced this fear to Al, "What if they take it out on Barbara?"

"They wouldn't dare!" he had said, pulling himself up to his full height. Sad as it is I have heard other parents admit to fears of retribution.

At this crucial time of Barbara's need for a new home, Karen, Barbara and I visited several in the general neighborhood with which she had become familiar. Each time Barbara had a succinct way of explaining why she did *not* like this house and each time we were unanimous. My yardstick question has always been, "Would I want to live there myself?" and in none of the homes we saw could I answer "yes."

At one point I tried to reassure Barbara by telling her of the many poor people who sleep in tents, broken down buildings, or under bridges. "You will never be without a home," I said. "Karen and I will see to that." A few days later she phoned Karen and wondered how she might meet some of those homeless people that Lotte has been talking about. "I would like to invite one or two of them to my birthday party in December." In the face of months of betrayal by our system Barbara still hoped and trusted.

Eventually — towards the end of the year — the bureaucracy bent on a point of contention and Barbara was able to move into the house in the country that she liked. At first all went well, but then we heard grumbles and rumbles from Barbara. "I miss Fred," she said, and we heard the same from him. As often as possible we arranged for the two of them to spend time together — usually when one or the other of their roommates was away for the weekend. It was an awkward arrangement because there was no public transportation from his house to hers, and the house van was not always available for these weekend visits. We heard about that too. Barbara missed riding the public bus which represented adult status to her.

That is when it became clear to us all that Fred and Barbara really wanted to be close to each other and that we were violating their right to a relationship by keeping them apart.

There came another move to another home where they could be together, but this turned out to be a nightmarishly bad situation which Gail and Chas and Karen and I watched with misgivings.

It was a spotlessly neat house, but there was little caring warmth in the caretaker's heart and we could not bear it any longer. It was another example of Barbara's stalwart endurance under duress.

And this is when Chas and Gail came to the rescue. Chas administered a group of small homes for young persons with developmental disabilities who also have some difficult behavioral and emotional problems. His wife, Gail, is licensed to operate a community care home. She grew up with a brother who has severe multiple disabilities and so she really understands and cares. My mentor, Professor Dybwad put it in a nutshell in a recent interview. He calls it a "language problem" and adds: "There is a world of difference between care and caring. Care is a bureaucratic term while caring is a human quality."

At this time Gail and Chas and their two children were living in the group home Gail was managing. It would be a little crowded, they said, but they really wanted to make it work for Barbara and Fred, and thought the two of them could live together in this house. And so it became their home.

They seemed to become a mutually supportive couple. When Fred had an accident with his bike and injured his back, Barbara worried and faithfully visited him in the hospital. He is always ready with his hand outstretched when Barbara has trouble negotiating stairs or difficult terrain. Fred had a job washing dishes at Mary's Pizza Parlor and Barbara began work in a fine training center with a wonderful director. In the house on Isabel Drive they had a room to themselves with a door they could close, and after a while they bought a queen size bed out of Fred's earnings and their Supplemental Social Security income. We celebrated their togetherness with a fine party at his work place.

Not long after their move, the Licensing Department came for a regular inspection. When they saw Barbara's and Fred's room they protested. "This conjugal arrangement has not been written into their program plan and must be stopped immediately," said the licensing inspector, and in spite of Gail's protest that they had just bought this bed and would probably be unwilling to saw it apart, the licensing report was passed on to the Regional Center. A sensitive and sensible Regional Center Counselor rescued them with a two and a half line letter on official stationery which stated: "Barbara Moise and Fred Waitt live at Gail Abate's house at 7670 Isabel in Cotati, and share a bedroom." Period! We never heard from licensing again, so I did not have to take the matter to the Supreme Court.

This was nine years ago and they have considered themselves a couple ever since and have often spoken of marriage, but there have been road blocks. The reduction of their monthly SSI payments is one of them. Once when the three of us were driving along I asked Fred *why* he wanted to be married. In his not so clear speech he said he wants to have babies. From the back seat Barbara spoke up firmly, "I can't have babies, Fred, you know that," and we talked for quite a few miles about it.

"You have your job at Mary's Pizza, Fred, and you love it. Who's going to take care of the baby?" I asked him.

His one-word answer was, "Barbara!"

She came right back: "But I want to work too!" and that sort of cooled the conversation.

The two of them really complement each other's skills. Fred is much more aggressive, independent and intelligent in some ways than Barbara, but she talks more clearly and that gives her an edge in many situations — such as on buses, in stores and on the phone. They have long conversations and she understands what he says often when I don't. Then I have to ask Barbara to "translate." Fred's number and money concepts are stronger. Neither of them can really read, but recognize a lot of so-called "survival" words and symbols like McDonalds. Barbara knows a few essential phone numbers by heart and can dial them.

Both of them have had speech therapy. I wish it could have come earlier for them. Today, since we know more about Down Syndrome, we could make a difference in Fred's communication skills. We now check for hearing deficits early in the lives of babies with Down Syndrome. Professor Doug Biklen of Syracuse University, *the* proponent of Facilitated Communication, has found that *early* teaching of signing and typing is extremely valuable for kids with "failed communication." (Suggested reading: Biklen, *Communication Unbound.*)

Barbara has definitely benefited from speech therapy. She is lazy about building complete sentences, but at times she comes out with a whopper in the strangest places. Karen, Barbara, Fred and I were having supper in a Thai restaurant and ordered soup. The soup was sort of whitish and very, very hot. Even Karen who likes hot food left part of hers. We all did. The nice young waitress came to remove our plates and as she did Barbara came out with perhaps the longest sentence of her life. Slowly and clearly she said: "The soup's too hot — pause — we didn't finish it — pause — it looks like something somebody did on the toilet." We all exploded with laughter.

There has been a steady increase in Fred's and Barbara's language development and communication skills over the years. I need fewer translations from Barbara of what Fred has said. They continue to give us and her house counselors insights into the depth of their understanding of and concern for the world they live in. They come out like sudden puffs of steam from an active crater.

Recently Barbara asked, "Why do people have to get killed in a war?" and, "Lotte, what's May Day?" Yesterday she barged into her house in the afternoon with a bright, "My name is Pollywog!"

(Suggested reading: Michael Berube's *Life As We Know It, A Father, a Family and an Exceptional Child.* In it he treats the puzzling and difficult subject of the acquisition of language. Berube is 36. His boy Jamie who has Down Syndrome is now six years old. I don't want to steal Michael's thunder, so I'll just tell you what he told me on the phone. He worked harder on the policy issues that concern his child —from I.Q. testing to social justice— than for his Ph.D. with which he teaches English at the University of Illinois. And he never loses sight of Jamie's development.)

On the surface Barbara and Fred's situation at their house appears to be unchanged. There have been some conversations with Fred and with the "little girl" who sought him out and so upset Barbara. Recently they have both begun to talk about getting married again. On the one hand I breathed a sigh of relief about their renewed togetherness. On the other hand there looms another hurdle. It's not only Fred and his roving eye, and Barbara reciprocating by teasing him about guys at work who like *her*. I consider that normal! The hurdle is the marriage penalty which casts a shadow on many couples who want to confirm their love "like normal people." Until recently some states still had laws on the books which categorically forbade marriages between persons with developmental disabilities. That's bad enough. But the "penalty" which inflicts a substantial reduction of the Social Security benefits to a married couple also threatens their medical benefits. It's based on the assumption that two people together can get by on less money than a single person. A ridiculous denial of reality — especially in a population which tends to have more medically necessary and expensive needs.

The *Protection and Advocacy Newsletter* of 1990 published this statement by John, a self-advocate:

> Frieda and I met about ten years ago, when we lived in a group home in Linthicum, Maryland. After we were seeing each other for about two years, we fell in love and wanted to get married. All my sisters and brothers are married. All Frieda's sisters and brothers are married. We wanted to get married because we are in love. But Frieda's family says we couldn't get married, my family says we couldn't get married, our agency says we couldn't get married.
>
> But Frieda and I don't give up. Every program coordinator we had, we asked, 'Can Frieda and I get married?' Finally we got a coordinator who says, 'Why not?' We talked with Frieda's family and they said, O.K. and Frieda's niece said, "I'll help." My family said no. We say, "We are going to get married anyway."
>
> My program coordinator came by with some bad news. She said if we get married, we won't get separate checks totaling $756 each month, but one check for both of us for $553 each month. We cannot afford that. We always dreamed of getting married in a church, but getting married in a church — we need a license. If we got married in a church, Frieda

would lose one of her checks. We got married anyway, without a license. We had a beautiful wedding in Down's Park with over 100 guests. Why couldn't we get married legally?

I know that Barbara and Fred echo his question. So I have to face the uncomfortable fact that from time to time my parental, underestimating, doubting Thomas still rears his head, and I need to shore up my belief in the commitment these two have given to each other in their non-verbal ways. Here I am — the widow who knew love, touch and closeness with my good husband for thirty-five years — still doubting that my daughter's feelings are any less real than were mine.

When in doubt, all I need to do is to review the video tape of our interview on Bay Area talk show *People Are Talking* in 1989. Our appearance on the hour long show was on the right to privacy and intimate relationships for persons with developmental disabilities. Can you imagine the surprise of a general audience to find this as the subject of their favorite morning talk show?

This is how Barbara and Fred and I became involved. Several young people who lived in a California State Development Center had contacted the State's Protection and Advocacy organization and lodged a complaint that they had absolutely no privacy in their lives to relate to their boyfriends or girlfriends. Somehow this came to the attention of Lynn Stigall-Muccigrosso, a co-worker of mine who is a professional trainer in the area of sexuality for staff people and for persons with disabilities. She had worked with the television station before. They became interested in the subject and the producer phoned me. Lynn had told her I had a daughter with a disability who was living with her boyfriend in a community home and she asked if we could be part of the program. My first reaction was a flat, "No." I explained to the producer that Fred has poor speech, and that I didn't think Barbara could handle a talk show interview either. I did however say I might reconsider my emphatic "No" if we could assemble a group of people with varied experiences. I recommended a young woman whom I had met at conferences on sexuality. I had learned to admire her and the zeal with which she talked about her right to love and have relationships. Lynn recommended two other persons, and then we were, from left to right, Mother Lotte, Barbara, Fred, Lynn the trainer, an older couple who were married and whose baby daughter had been taken away because of the mother's disability, and Pam the feisty young advocate.

It worked beautifully. Once again I had underestimated Barbara's and Fred's ability to come across with few words. They were wonderful. They communicated. The cameras did a sensitive job and the interviewers were tremendous. Of course we were all dressed in our best bib and tucker, and were made to look glamorous with professional make-up.

The interviewers — a man and a woman — waded right into the core of my fears for Barbara when she was just a baby. Would she be able to get married and have children? I was able to handle that one. But then they squarely tackled the fact that Barbara had had a tubal ligation. Out of the corner of my eyes — or from my motherly intuition — I sensed that Barbara must feel uncomfortable. The videotape confirms this by the look on her face. So I parried that question. I acknowledged it with a "yes" and then turned the question to Barbara and asked her if she really wanted to talk about this on television. "No!" she said with a firm shake of the head and grabbed Fred's hand. The camera zoomed in on them several more times and each time their joined hands spoke more clearly than words.

Of course we were all proud and excited and basked in our TV fame. The video has become a useful training tool for me. Not only does it introduce Barbara and Fred when I speak about them; it also discusses some of the more difficult aspects of the subject of sexuality, and attempts to allay the fears that "teaching about sexuality will promote promiscuity and pregnancies." Lynn emphasizes that carefully prepared social training *and information* are vitally necessary for our people, and she illustrates it with clips from some of her training sessions with young adults in school and work settings. Pam echoes her points with vigorous statements about irresponsible behaviors of so-called "normal" people. She drew the loudest applause from the studio audience!

Fred and Barbara are among the lucky ones — for now. They do have family and friends. Barbara's loyalty to family and friends knows no bounds, and she remembers and would like to hold on to small holiday traditions from her early childhood. Like the gingerbread boys for Halloween and pastry Easter bunnies and colored eggs for Easter that we used to construct, and for which my enthusiasm has waned!

When she was a very small girl Al and I met a couple by the name Moise who lived in Southern California and they visited us at our house. We tried to figure out if we might be related but couldn't, and eventually lost track of each other. Barbara has never forgotten this and occasionally asks about them as if she felt deprived of the connection. It's hard for me to explain to her how one can lose touch. There *is* a group of former Fort Bragg friends whose work lives have moved them to other towns and with whom we hold reunions. Barbara refers to these as "family reunions," and looks forward to them with anticipation.

Once David took a family photo of us all and I had it transferred and put on a T-shirt for Barbara. Fred was in the photo with us and protested clearly when he didn't get a shirt like it. He got one on the next festive occasion. And when I introduce Barbara to new friends Fred's hand is right out there with, "and me Fred!" He definitely considers himself part of our family.

Outings and adventures are a part of Fred and Barbara's life as well. There is Dodie, mother of their good friend Jeff, who recently died and for whom they both grieve. Dodie is now a travel agent and organizes group trips for young persons with disabilities — once to Hawaii, other times to Disney Land, Knott's Berry Farm, and recently a four-day caravan by car to Gold Beach and the Rogue River in Oregon. A friend and I drove one of the cars with Barbara and Fred as our passengers. Both of them were well organized travelers. On the last evening of our journey they asked to go to the restaurant in the motel by themselves and proudly sat at their own table — ordered their food and grinned at us from a distance. We only helped them slightly when it came to the check and the tip.

When Al was still alive, Barbara experienced a couple of big trips to Europe with us. She insisted on coming along. "I want to see my friends in Denmark again" — the ones she had met in 1971 during our Dybwad fellowship travel grant. "And my cousins." My brother and his family were posted in Vienna by the Foreign Service. Both trips involved demanding itineraries with trains that wobbled and a ship that rolled and pitched. She was scared but overcame her fears and never missed a meal in the dining car or dining room.

Often I was amazed. Often I am still amazed, but I have a good friend who is also a close friend to both Barbara and Fred, who stops me. "It's out of keeping of your growing-up-with-Barbara philosophy," he'll say, "You shouldn't be amazed." And he's right.

Peope Are Talking (KPIX, 1989)

163

Pie a la Fred

And she loves babies!

Chapter 13

Hurdles of Health, Acceptance and Permanency

The road Barbara has traveled since I wrote her first book has not been a smooth one, and more and more I admire the courage with which she overcomes the hurdles of living with a developmental disability. She wished that she could read "like David and Karen," and there's her poor coordination, her fight to keep her weight under control, her fear of escalators. Yet she *is* one of the lucky ones. Lucky because she lives in California where, long ago in the sixties, we created an entitlement program called the Lanterman Act which used to be the envy of other states. Sadly, it is now in danger of being eroded and steamrollered by the budget-cutting zealots in Washington and by its own bureaucratic weight and complexity.

Just last year Barbara had a bout of vertigo. We don't know exactly what caused it. The physical exam was inconclusive, but her balance isn't good in the first place, and she became so afraid of falling that it virtually immobilized her for weeks. Open spaces especially "froze" her. In wide store aisles and sunny streets without close-by houses she'd grab her pants legs, stop still, shriek, and wouldn't move until one of us gave her a hand or an arm for support. I began to have nightmares that she might become non-ambulant. Once or twice she asked about getting a wheelchair. But the staff people in her program slowly and gently helped her overcome much of her fear. Fred was, if

165

anything, over-protective, and Barbara too dependent on him. He drove me to yell at him, "Let her try it by herself!" She is still not as agile as she was some years ago but courageously she keeps trying. I so empathize with her for I can remember my own fears on the diving board, panicky moments on narrow trails in the mountains, and Karen and David's first attempts on bikes and skates and stilts. As a family we don't seem to be a very athletic bunch.

There are other health hurdles for her. She has recently developed asthma and takes her pills and uses her inhaler device with little prompting. Fred is her back-up reminder on this too.

She was born with really bad feet and has to have special orthotics in her shoes. For a while she had to wear a brace on one knee which required twice-a-day on and off maneuvering. On one shopping trip — many years ago — we had patiently tried many shoes and had to settle for a plain clonky pair. She burst out in frustration, "I want red, pretty shoes!" It's a good thing that current fashionable foot wear leans heavily towards high top hiking shoes, so she's positively and proudly stylish in her boots.

As with many of our sons and daughters who live in their home communities or close by, it is the social and recreational part of their lives which presents a problem, and the more they reach for the so-called pinnacle of accomplishment, namely "a place of their own," the more I fear that we will have many lonely people. We try. For those who have elected to move into their own apartments, or homes, we establish a new layer of staff persons for personal support. These may be live-in roommates who chose to help with obstacles of daily living on an ongoing basis and share the rent and household expenses. Often they are college students. Or, the umbrella agency (in California the network of twenty-one Regional Centers) trains and provides staff persons for daily living support for as many hours of the week as needed. We have established "Circles of Friends" consisting of family members, neighbors and friends who surround the person for purposes of planning for their support needs. In some states neighborhood drop-in centers have been created. Here in California we are working hard at such supported living arrangements but I am afraid that we are creating another layer of bureaucracy in an already complex system of community supports. As a mother I don't feel assured of stability, and *fall back provisions* as the natural aging process changes and increases the need for security for our sons and daughters, as it does for all of us.

This Thanksgiving weekend was a true example of "neighborhood" at its best. A young woman who lives in our small town's group home for six young men and women lost her mother recently. She has no other family near by, so the director of the home invited her to her home to have Thanksgiving dinner with her family. A young man in my daughter's home in Cotati is totally on his own, and he too was invited by the director of his house.

Clearly that is the way it ought to be. Years ago when we first put in place California's system of twenty-one Regional Centers and its hundreds of employees, we worried about who would be there for our people on festive and sad occasions after we are gone. Naively we thought of Regional Centers as an extended family and are now finding that it's not as simple as all that. How to foster independence and also provide emotional and social supports remain difficult goals to accomplish. The striving for a place of one's choosing and of one's own is still a lofty ideal on the road to total community integration, but let us not delude ourselves. Integration is a sham if it does not result in participation — real participation in clubs, recreation centers, committees, bowling leagues and other civic activities. The holiday seasons clearly show me that we need still more Community.

Both Barbara and Fred are warmly sociable persons, but need guidance in structuring appropriate and accessible activities for themselves for their free time after work and on weekends. They visit Karen often in San Francisco. Bruce, another housemate, sometimes comes along; he has a family, but they deny his existence and have gone on record that they don't want to hear about him; his siblings don't know he exists so Gail and Chas have become his family, and his security rests in them. Barbara and Fred's first solo venture to the city by Golden Gate Transit public transportation turned out to be a traumatic affair for Karen. She had given them instructions to take the bus to the end of the line — a large transit terminal in downtown San Francisco. They weren't in the place where she had told them to wait. She panicked — wandered around and was about to contact the police when she spotted them — unconcerned in a slightly different spot. "When I recovered I fixed that once and for all." Karen told me. "I bought them a hamburger at a lunch counter right then and there and informed them that this would now be the meeting place!" The reinforcement worked like a charm! Since then they have settled on a better place. It's a good sheltered spot at the south end of the Golden Gate Bridge where Karen can park her car and they have a pay phone handy if needed.

They have wonderful times together in San Francisco. Shopping (for shoes for Barbara's difficult feet) and Chinese food are high on the list, but they also explore the city which Karen has learned to love. And I think Barbara has moved Karen to the top of the list of people she depends on for security — even higher than Fred, or David's family, or me, for in my case she is so aware that I too may die like her Dad.

When Fred and Barbara come up to visit me for the weekend, their plans are flexible. Sometimes Fred stays at his family's house — a few blocks away. He especially likes being there when there are little cousins visiting. But he enjoys doing things with Barbara and me and Karen, and he often joins us for meals and activities. Over major holidays like Thanksgiving and Christmas he's liable to have two dinners in a row — one at his place and one with us. When it's crowded at his house he just brings his suitcase and moves in with us. I am the one who meets them at the bus. Fred's Dad gathers them up for the early morning bus departure.

Fred's stepmother recently died. It was a hard time for us all, for Fred was so desperately sad during the entire process of her illness and then her death. We tried to explain the inevitability of death to him, and with his incomplete speech he was able to say how bereft he felt. His dad was in the hospital with pneumonia at the same time, and Fred asked "Who is there now for me? You?" pointing to Karen and to me. It was heartbreaking.

Now that Mr. Waitt is a widower, he has moved into a small cottage where there is just room enough for Fred to roll out his sleeping bag in a corner. He and Barbara then call each other in the morning and decide what to do: yard sales or TV football games for Fred with his dad, or shopping and visiting their many old friends for Barbara, Fred and me. Last Christmas his father took him to Texas to visit relatives for a week. They had a great time together but Barbara didn't like the idea a bit. She missed him terribly and it was difficult to convince her that there are times when there can be spaces in their togetherness.

When they are at their group home in Cotati, Fred will strike out and walk to visit neighbors and to buy himself a coke (he's addicted to cokes). Barbara doesn't like to venture forth on her own, and neither of them are great at making a real attempt to arrange visits with people in the area that they do know. Thank goodness the staff counselors are there to help organize group outings. Were they to move into a place of their own I fear they would be lonely — even with the best of support services from their Regional Centers (currently running at a substantial deficit and cutting back on services) and with organized "Circles of Friends." Even the frequent Fort Bragg weekends and trips to Karen's in San Francisco do not happen often and regularly enough. Fred is more inclined to head out alone. Barbara — when she is bored — turns on television and sticks her thumb in her mouth. She needs a lot of social interaction. As do many of us.

The entire matter of recreation and social integration into community also depends a great deal on available transportation. Public buses must be available and accessible — not only during the week and in day time, but at hours on weekends and in the evening when the need for recreation is most urgent for potentially lonesome folk. We have a long way to go, and I never thought I would get involved in this issue, but I have.

Fort Bragg is naturally isolated from urban centers by crooked mountainous roads. It's a three hour drive from here to where Barbara and Fred live in Cotati, and one more to reach the Bay Area. When Greyhound abandoned many small towns nationwide, we too got the ax and I found that their trip home by public transportation became difficult and confusing. It also literally pulled the wheels out from under many senior citizens. A private entrepreneur ran a small van for a while, but that service died by attrition, and I found myself advocating for a county bus service — not only for my kids — but for the many other disabled, elderly and car-less persons on our Coast. Recently our public Mendocino Transit Authority established a small, daily bus from here to Santa Rosa, and coast residents can now keep medical and business appointments and make airport connections. Barbara and Fred ride this bus, and it's a happy improvement, but we must now encourage ridership to ensure its continuation.

Meaningful integration also involves meaningful work. Fred is great at making eggs and toast for his own breakfast. I have recently discovered that my daughter is good at flipping pancakes, and since my hand tremor tends to land the flapjacks on the ceiling, that's a big help. They can both put together a good fruit salad. Fred also likes to stack wood for our wood stove and they team up for this chore, with Fred being a vocal boss. They then proudly remind me that "wood work" is a reimbursable activity.

Until recently Fred considered himself a professional dishwasher at Mary's Pizza and he had proudly worked there for close to 15 years. There used to be no holding him when it was time to go to work on Monday. Now he was dragging his feet. A new rule at Mary's Pizza cooled his enthusiasm. He now had to bring his own lunch instead of eating on the job. Meals are very important to Fred, and since this change directly affected his stomach he sulked and grouched. It was time for a change.

And Fred was bored. Chas, Gail, Karen and I agreed, and now he is working at a furniture manufacturing company with a team of five of his peers and a supervisor. He tells me he likes it and is once more a happy fellow.

Barbara, who has known the value of money since she was a little girl, recently began to set her hopes on "a real job." I am sure that Fred's long-time employment and his enthusiasm for going to work rubbed off on her. She seemed highly motivated, and so the staff at her Work Training Center enrolled her in a Rehab Program which consisted of several short-term trial assessment placements.

The first one was to be at Burger King, fairly conveniently located on a very busy street right across from the junior college campus. Barbara was wildly excited. When I asked her if she knew what she would be doing, she promptly listed wiping tables and emptying the garbage, and she seemed impressed with the uniform she'd be wearing. The great day came for the first interview. Barbara commented to the manager, "There are lots of people here."

"Yes, Barbara, and what will you do when it gets crowded?"

"Tell 'em to go home," was her simple solution. She didn't get that job.

The next placement might have worked out. At least we got good reports from Barbara's job coach. She worked at a nursing home and helped with the recreation program for some of the older ladies. She played Bingo with them, poured juice, and did a bit of physical therapy. She was throwing a soft ball back and forth to one woman who hardly ever spoke. When Barbara dropped the ball, the woman was heard to say loud and clear, "Butterfingers!" Apparently quite a breakthrough for her, and another woman said, "We like Barbara, I think we'll keep her!"

But then Barbara blew it. She was pushing a woman in a wheelchair down the crowded corridor and ran into a traffic jam. "Why don't you get up and walk?" suggested my daughter. The woman tried to get up and, thank goodness, sat right down again, but someone saw this and Barbara was terminated. The job coach broke it to me rather gently. She said that they had terminated her for too much initiative (we wonder where she got this?) and not enough judgment. But Barbara isn't one for euphemisms. When she called me that evening she said, "I got fired, Lotte." We talked about it. From my long-ago experience in vocational counseling I could tell her that it's not the end of the world — that she probably learned from the experience — that I too got fired once in my life. She was sad though. She really liked the work, and the job coach and Karen and I all thought the staff should have trained her in more detail than they did.

It was then that I asked Barbara to tell me the things she would most like about a "real job" and she came up with the following specifics: she'd like to wear a uniform, she'd like to work sitting down, she preferred working indoors, and for people not to stare at her.

She was ready to give the community work program one more try. This one was a trial run at a Red Lobster restaurant. The transportation connection to her work place was a bit risky but it would be a test of her hand skills (which are good) and her concentration. It was to be a two hour task — in the mornings — rolling the day's supply of silverware into napkins.

At first all went well, but then we heard that our sociable Barbara was so fascinated by the beautiful red lobsters in the tank that she would stop to watch and talk to them as she went back and forth to pick up her supplies. This California kid had never seen live lobsters before. She also socialized with the nice waitresses and they had not been specifically instructed to tell Barbara to get back to her work table.

There was a follow-up meeting on this work experience. Barbara was center stage surrounded by her support team — a person from her house, from her work center, the job coach, Karen, Lotte and the counselors from the Department of Rehabilitation. It's a process Barbara enjoys in spite of criticism, because all the people involved are supportive and plugging for her. The Rehab counselors however tend to phrase their questions in rather technical language and I find myself having to ask them to keep them a bit more simple. When the meeting was winding down the last question for Barbara was, "What do you think you learned from this job?" She burst out laughing and said, "I tried to eat the fake cakes." She had tried another difficult task, and when it didn't work out, her delightful sense of humor pulled her through.

When she returned to the work training center and was assigned to a crew to do some rather routine piece work for a large electronic firm, she experienced vertigo attacks for the first time and was taken off that assignment. During those weeks she became belligerently unhappy, with real outbursts of temper. My charmingly radiant daughter was

"exhibiting" what in the jargon of the developmental disabilities service system is referred to as "behaviors" and that's "B A D." For Barbara
it was certainly very difficult to explain how she felt after her failure in
the three work assessment trials on which she had pinned her hopes
— and now this.

It was at times like this that I wished we could clone Herb Lovett,
a clinical psychologist in Boston — nationally known in the field —
who counsels with people like Barbara and her support staff to ferret
out what's behind angry outbursts so hard to put into words. By the
time I became fully aware of them, Barbara had become too "wobbly"
on her feet from vertigo for me to suggest that she take out her anger
with boxing gloves.

She's feeling better physically now. She seems content with her individual tutoring program. It is varied and she enjoys it. Her schedule
ranges from housecleaning (she attacks bathrooms with vigor) to
community outings that stretch her endurance with walking. There is
arts and crafts work — beautiful bead necklaces and designs on T-
shirts — that encourage her creative side and cause me motherly
pride. She earns a small check on payday.

The final major hurdle Barbara and all of us must clear is that of
permanency. Ask yourself, why do elderly people, especially those
who have lost a spouse, congregate in cooperative housing arrangements? And for that matter, why do non-elderly persons choose to
move into rooming houses? A recent article in the Newsletter of the
American Association of Retired Persons had an article entitled *Living
Together: Innovations Abound as Americans Experiment with Shared
Housing*. All of these arrangements seem designed to avoid loneliness.
One in Vermont is a large old house with 19 private rooms — each
with phone and cable TV hookups and a bathroom shared with one
other person. The main floor houses an adult day care center where
others from the community come for activities. Rent is $625 and in-
cludes meals for which everyone gathers.

Here in California we now have a mandate for innovative solutions
to living arrangements for our sons and daughters, based on their
wishes and coping abilities. My best wish for Barbara and Fred is a

mother-in-law place of their own — a hop skip and jump from a group home like the one in which she and Fred now have their room, with the space and privacy that they need, and close proximity to others with whom they can visit and who can assist them.

On the broader, national front public awareness of the *capabilities* of our citizens rather than their *disabilities* has increased considerably, and that is encouraging. I wish I could now switch from print to show-and-tell and roll a video produced and distributed in 1993: *Employability; Integrating People with Disabilities into the Workplace.* (Available free from the Woolworth Company, Kevin McLaughlin, Public Affairs, 233 Broadway, NY, NY 10279-0003). James Earl Jones introduces the film, and himself. "I work as an actor," he says, "an unlikely career choice because I have a problem with stuttering, so I have a disability." He continues by speaking of the persons in the video as being capable and good for business. then we see CEOs from Woolworth, AT&T, Johnson & Johnson and UPS who echo this statement and show their employees who have visible and audible disabilites as they are being trained and talk about their jobs. There are men and women with Down Syndrome, Cerebral Palsy, and in wheelchairs. One man uses a voice synthesizer.

Staff persons express their admiration for the workers and their persistence and steadfastness as they grow into their jobs. In the end one of the CEOs refers to his employees as valued citizens. The final shot is of a young man who says, "I want to be treated like everyone else — nice!"

It seems to me there is a very important component missing from planning in our state. In a program in Michigan they call it "permanency planning"; in Denmark in the seventies I found "fall-back" arrangements. When you lose a spouse you realize that there is really no "permanence" in anyone's life, but we owe it to our more fragile persons with disabilities to prepare for a "fall-back." If a relationship between a couple — be they married or compatible roommates — breaks up or changes, (and a broken hip or illness can cause this) we may find that the need for support increases immensely and immediately. What my husband did for me I now have to learn to do for myself, or to shift to someone else's shoulders. I look for such fall-back homes for some of our young people who are capable of a measure of independence *now*, but may at some time in the future find themselves more vulnerable because they are alone. "Independence" is a myth. Years ago the wise Bob Perske wrote about "inter-dependence," and I think there is much to be said for a combination of congregate living, as long as *individual* independence and autonomy are supported and fostered in such a setting.

The role changes resulting from aging (the French refer to us as "persons of the third age") are a reality we cannot ignore and must plan for.

Chapter 14

Are We Better Off?

So are "we" — the thousands of persons in this country who either live with a family member with a developmental disability, who know one, or who have such a disability ourselves — better off than we were when we began our "civil rights" movement? The answer is both "Yes" and "No."

It is still an uphill struggle to create honest-to-goodness supports and inclusive communities for the Barbaras of this world — even here in the rich, progressive United States, and in the Golden State of California. But there *are* exemplary models to learn from and horizons to shoot for — *and* persons with disabilities who can by now teach us a thing or two, if only we will listen.

In 1978 The President's Committee on Mental Retardation published a report entitled, *Mental Retardation: The Leading Edge — Service Programs that Work.* First Lady Rosalynn Carter had requested such information and The President's Committee enlisted the talents of Robert and Martha Perske to describe and illustrate some of these programs. Bob scurried throughout the country to see for himself. The book charged me with great optimism, but also with the realization that my map for the future of our sons and daughters was still far from covered by such excellence. But, as Bob assessed the situation, "It's like parts of the car are all over the garage floor. All we have to do now is put them together."

According to projections made by the President's Committee on

Mental Retardation at that time, the incidence of mental retardation could be cut in half by the end of the century if we practiced all we knew. If we could wipe out all layers of poverty, eliminate cultural deprivation, and provide love, security and care for all children, we would prevent many disabling conditions.

We *have* learned a great deal about pre-natal care, good nutrition, and prevention. For those families who already have a child with a developmental disability, genetic counseling is available for both parents and siblings. The mother can have an amniocentesis procedure and ultra-sound both of which diagnose certain abnormalities of the fetus inside the uterus.

I was thirty-five when I was pregnant with Barbara. I'm sure I would have availed myself of amniocentesis if it had been available in 1953, and if I had known that I was a mother at risk because of my age. But would I have chosen an abortion if I had been told of the possibility of an abnormality? It's impossible to second-guess a decision I did not have to make at the time.

It is precisely at this point that prevention becomes a difficult ethical question. Barbara is alive and a real person, and were I to have answered yes, it would have been like a retroactive death wish for a member of our family whom we love and value. Yet I firmly believe that biochemists and physicians will continue to ask why children are born with impairments, deformities and pathologies. They will continue to want to "prevent" these problems, in the dictionary sense of the word, to "forestall, hinder, keep from happening." I want the researchers to continue, for much as Barbara has deepened my awareness of the human condition and broadened my horizon, I also realize that she has been cheated of much pleasure, and I would have wished her a more trouble-free life.

Some of the young mothers of today are able to combine resignation to disability with high expectations. In the September 1996 *Networker,* a newsletter published by the Matrix Parent Network of California's Marin County, there is an article by Carol Gonsalves boldly entitled "Disability as a Part of Life." She writes:

When your child is diagnosed with a disability, whether it is at birth or later on, as a parent your life feels shattered, your heart aches in a way you never dreamed possible. That other parents share the same heartache seems quite removed. However, as we move forward and help our child be the best she can be, we begin to see how many other families and individuals are affected with disabilities. In fact, it becomes more apparent that disability is another fact of life, another variation in the human experience.

The experiences of parents are verified by statistical evidence. In a report by the California Birth Defects Monitoring Program, the largest analysis of birth defects undertaken, 1.6 million births between 1983 and 1990 were studied and little change in overall rates was found. This occurred despite an emphasis on prenatal care and widespread screening for two birth defects — Down syndrome and neural tube defects (spina bifida). In fact, birth defects are found to occur in one out of every 33 births. Teen mothers have an eleven percent higher risk for birth defects compared to mothers who are ages 20-29. It is also known that older mothers have a higher risk of having a baby with a birth defect.

So what does all this mean? It means that those who plan for our futures, who chart our medical paths, need to incorporate the knowledge that disability is a part of life. Whether it be legislators and government officials who negotiate provisions for special education or doctors and the medical community who oversee pregnancy, birth, childhood, and adulthood, disability must be viewed as part of who we are as human beings. Just as we plan for college, as we look to care for senior citizens, as we allow for differences in athletic ability, we need to make sure we plan to include those with disabilities "in the big picture" of our world. Birthday parties and playtime at the park, school projects and band class, vocational/career planning and weekends away, these are all activities in which those with disabilities can participate.

Ignoring the value of those with disabilities in all of the many activities in our communities, and assuming parents will terminate a pregnancy when it is determined that the baby has disabilities, these are all forms of discrimination. In our high speed rush to technological superiority and material preeminence, we must not forget who we are as people: individuals who come in all sizes, colors, abilities, and interests. Disability is a part of life, and we are obligated to insure that this message is never lost.

A British co-worker of mine reached a similar conclusion: "Mental Retardation? that's just the way some people are." A perfect logo for school and community inclusion.

A brilliant young social worker studying for her law degree said to me, "If my disability (spina bifida) had been discovered by amniocentesis they might have killed me."

Twenty-five years ago we were just beginning to receive information on medical research that might throw light on the causes for our children's medical conditions. At a state convention of parent associations, we were told by genetic experts that they had come up with new identifiable chromosomal information on mental retardation. They were encouraging us as "high risk" families to make use of this knowledge. Al and I decided to have a chromosomal study done which might throw some light on the cause of Barbara's condition. Her file referred to it simply as "etiology unknown."

If there was one thing Barbara hated, it was needles, but in our fervor to advance the cause of science we went ahead. This put us in the position of trying to explain to her why she had to let the doctor take some blood out of her arm and send it to the lab. We didn't want to say that there was something wrong with her or that we wouldn't want Karen or David to run the risk of having a child like her. But she had let us know that she was aware of her problems with speech, physical coordination and reading, so we told her that the blood test might tell doctors why she had these problems, and then they might be able to help new babies grow up without them. Barbara seemed to accept this explanation, but the tests showed no chromosomal abnormalities.

The Association for Retarded Children (which later changed its name from Children to Citizens and is now called The Arc), and those of us who belonged to it, eagerly continued to work for the cause of medical research. From small local chapters to state organizations up to national headquarters, we made significant financial contributions to medical research each year at convention time, and spread the word about new-found knowledge. Then we used all possible political muscle to push for and demand preventive measures.

I especially remember the annual State Convention of 1968 when Dr. Richard Koch was President of the California Association. He was at the time a practicing professor of pediatrics and strong advocate for our children. He spoke to us of his research on PKU (phenylketonuria), a metabolic disease in which a faulty gene causes a build-up of the amino acid phenylalanine (contained in all protein foods like milk and meat) in the blood of the baby. This failure of the body to handle protein will result in serious mental retardation and autism by the age of three if not immediately treated with a stringent diet. Dr. Koch explained that the test could be done by drawing a single drop of blood taken from the heel of a newborn. Then he urged us to "hit the pavement" and talk to our local physicians about this. At first we protested that as lay-person-parents we wouldn't get past the receptionist without explanations in hand. If I remember correctly we subsequently received such factual information. Then we did go out to tackle our local doctors, and the "heel test" for PKU is now being done routinely for all newborns in the United States and Canada. Stringent diet for the first eight years of life was shown to inhibit developmental delays.

But medical research on PKU has not stood still. Barbara Dolan, Nurse Counselor for Genetics of Redwood Coast Regional Center, the center for our four-county Northern California area, tells me Dr. Koch has continued his work on PKU and has made life saving new discoveries. He has found evidence that some of the PKU babies who were allowed to go off the special diet at eight years of age are showing increased levels of phenylalaline in adulthood with disturbing symptoms. The thought of resuming the distasteful diet which over-shadowed their childhood is frightening but necessary. It is especially necessary and doubly scary for women who are pregnant, because, if their phenylalanine level has risen to abnormally high levels, it may endanger the fetus.

Dr. Koch, Barbara Dolan, and Christina Bekins, a nutrition consultant, are now jointly preparing a paper on treatment interventions for those persons of advanced age who were never tested for or treated for PKU as babies. The two examples of their study are women in their upper fifties who have significant developmental disabilities and are developing additional symptoms extremely difficult to manage for those who take care of them. But even at this late stage in their lives they are showing great improvement with dietary intervention and so-cial/psychological support.

Dr. Koch continues his work as participant in the Division of Medical Genetics at Children's Hospital of the University of Southern California in Los Angeles. He has recently made it his mission to lo-cate former PKU patients and alert them to these new developments in order to prevent problems in a new generation of babies.

Parents have continued their personal involvement in other pre-vention issues. We pushed for stricter regulations and greater aware-ness of the dangers of lead poisoning, and the urgent need for a full range of immunizations for all children. These trojan efforts made a difference in early diagnosis and intervention, and have improved the quality of life for children. The attitude of society has changed be-cause of our early efforts. More people truly believe that these babies' lives will be worth living — and that they will be valued — as it should be. That is progress, and as members of a parent movement we can take pride in it.

All these medical research efforts have gradually led us from the relatively narrow term "mental retardation" to the broader "develop-mental disabilities." It's still a tongue twister for some people, but is based on practical observations. "Mental retardation" can take many shapes, and encompasses a wide range of conditions from mild "slow learning" that is hardly noticeable, to severe combinations of medical diagnoses that overlap in treatment and interventions. thus "develop-mental disabilities" became the umbrella term. It was developed in the Congressional Kennedy-Yarborough bill, and was to include Cerebral Palsy, Epilepsy, later Autism and other neurological disorders that can benefit from similar programs. At the time individual advocacy or-ganization worried about losing their hard fought identities and fi-

nancial support by the broadened terminology. We tended to be paro-
chially protective of the boundaries of our advocacy efforts.

Personally I hoped this might lead to the Scandinavian approach
that I had experienced, and which in the early seventies was focused
on specific needs, regardless of diagnosis. A wheelchair was a wheelchair, and made available whether the person needed it temporarily
for a ski fracture, or for a life with severe cerebral palsy. Sadly we still
haven't streamlined our efforts. California's definition of developmental disability is different from the federal one. The federal definition is
based on "daily living functioning," while in California we base eligi-
bility for services on categorical diagnostic categories. It's confusing
and persons with problems do fall between the cracks.

But parents do not give up. They have created wonderful oases
which Bob Perske eloquently described in 1978 in his *The Leading
Edge* report. He stoked our optimism and resolve to become the first
line of defense for our children.

Take for instance an ideal situation. A baby is born with a disability. Help is available right after the baby is born because medical and
nursing personnel have been well trained in counseling parents. Instead of postponing the discussion or glossing over the problem, the
physician gently but honestly breaks the news to both mother and father. There is no longer any talk of placing the baby out of the home
to spare the siblings. At this moment both parents may be incapable
of understanding scientific explanations, but they can feel warmth
and caring.

Enter Pilot Parents. They have been there themselves. They have
been trained to listen, to comfort, and to know available resources. If
the newborn has been diagnosed as having Down Syndrome parents
can meet young persons who have that condition, who can explain
how it feels and describe what they themselves have accomplished.
The new parents will be able to place trust in future supports and resources in their community. The team approach begins. I know of one
father who almost immediately after the birth of his child, picked up
the phone and joined such a support organization.

The Leading Edge described examples of situations that made my own problems with Barbara seem insignificant. One couple, parents of a profoundly handicapped son and two teenage daughters, founded a home here in California called the Somerset Home School. It became a twenty-four hour training unit for six severely handicapped youngsters. The father and mother were administrator and program director and they employed four child care workers. Their home had access to the services of a physical therapist, nutritionist, case workers from the California Regional Center of their area, and a registered nurse. It became far more than a place where services were delivered. According to *The Leading Edge:*

> Frail, multi-handicapped children come into a three-acre wonderland of sensory stimulation and the reinforcement of healthy responses to it. The house is filled with bright colors, harmonious music, restful waterbeds, voices with loving tones, hands that massage, arms that hold one close, the stimulating waters of a Jacuzzi whirlpool, the smell of bread and a noisy canary. Outside is the sun, fresh air, a swimming pool, two spirited horses, a gentle pony, goats, dogs, cats, a rabbit and a duck, All play an important part in giving direction to these children's lives.

The training program itself was intense:

> Detailed interventions of Neurodevelopmental Training are carried out faithfully. For example, body positioning and head control programs continue all day. The jerky infantile reflexes — so important at birth but an impediment to growth if they fail to diminish — are helped to fade, while the purposeful use of lips, tongue and jaw are stimulated and reinforced... All efforts are geared to helping the children move from weakness to strength, from negative behaviors to purposeful interactions with the world around them. Their progress is measured by precision charting of behaviors, as well as by monthly videotapes.

The aim of Somerset Home School was to provide every appropriate early childhood intervention and to involve the family increasingly so that a stronger, more valued child would return to his or her own home. In his glowing report on the program Robert Perske cast a vote for parental action:

> There is hope for the mentally retarded [1978 language] when

the parents of such children refuse to accept what others believe about their handicapped child. In this case, a family has ignored the pessimistic presumptions that profoundly handicapped children must be written off as having no future at all... Salvaging destinies is a supremely difficult business but it can be done.

The Leading Edge became a yardstick for me. Perske's book assured me that the programs I dreamed of for Barbara and her friends actually existed out there. That there were others who, regardless of the severity of their children's disabilities and level of functioning, believed they were worthy of excellence.

It has been eighteen years since *The Leading Edge* was published, and I had often wondered what happened to the Somerset Home School and the family who founded it. Did they still exist? Would their work still be an inspiration to parents? So I picked up the phone. The family's story has taken a sharp turn. Their marriage ended in divorce. Their son with severe disability lived to be nine years old, but the seed core of dedication remained intact in the mother. Her two daughters are grown and married, and as she says, "They are both wonderful mothers." She herself has become trained in the Waldorf method of education, and now that she is remarried, has founded another *Somerset School* with her new husband. At present it is a day school but they plan to enroll two live-in students. Again the school is located on many acres of beautiful land with all the stimulation of animals, gardens and water, as before. The school is staffed by trained Waldorf teachers and privately funded. The students have a range of learning disabilities, but are not as severely disabled as those in the previous school. Vitality, energy and joy were in her voice as we talked, and I was convinced that her and her husband's work comes under the "YES" column of my "are we better off?" question. Though she is not connected with our State of California's Developmental Disabilities System, she *is* bettering the lives of children with special needs. Robert Perske can be proud of her.

The Leading Edge also covered prevention, early intervention, infant stimulation and home training for parents. Infant stimulation included motor, language, and play activities which help a child "learn to move" so that he and she can "move to learn." We had stumbled on to the right track in our own attempts at stimulation for Barbara and I wish we had done more.

Perske's book reminded me of our own family's early start. We had been so lucky living in a friendly, rural community, complete with two parents, two siblings, good neighbors close by and a circle of friends. *Respite*— the chief ingredient in care for a child with developmental problems was then, and still is now, hard to come by and frequently missing. We were lucky to have had it.

It is inexcusable and discouraging that parents are still having difficulties in launching respite programs. There is an expressed need for this service, and I consider it *the* cornerstone of success of community programs, but at times it is the families themselves who are reluctant to ask for it. I have thoughts about the reasons why. Frequently the service agencies are responsible when they fail to let parents know respite is available. That's unconscionable. But parents may be too proud to ask. They are stuck in the stiff-upper-lip-do-it-yourself philosophy until something in the family constellation cracks. Both parents may be holding jobs. The pressure of all the activities which are focused on the child with special needs becomes overwhelming. Nobody smiles anymore. There seems to be no time for picnics or weekend outings. No one talks about Little League or soccer. And for the married couple it's goodbye to dancing, bridge or dinner out with friends. Even a normally relaxed sex life may seem unattainable.

I vividly remember the day I decided Karen and David were old enough to keep an eye on Barbara while I took a bath with the door closed. It was a memorable occasion. And I met a mother who had finally managed to enroll her little girl in public school in her neighborhood. I heard her burst out, "Goodbye advocacy! Hello world!" and she went on to say that she had just signed up for an art class at the junior college. Hers is just one small example of the creative energy that can be released in families through respite, and that is why it is so vitally important. It enables families to lead as normal a life as possible before stress, tensions and fatigue undermine relationships. Respite support should be offered freely to those who need it. Nobody should be made to feel guilty about asking for it. In time, such a family may become a pillar of strength for others. I am learning in my own "third age" that asking for help can be a sign of strength.

The most visible changes in public services since Barbara was a little girl — and still the most controversial — are in the areas of education, employment and access to essential locations in home communities. Even in my glummest moments I can take comfort in that.

In education we survived the hard-fought era of "mainstreaming" which enabled our children to attend school on regular campuses, though not truly integrated into classrooms or activities with their peers. It was the trailer-at-the-far-end-of-the-campus-syndrome. The opposition by teachers and administrators to the concept was based on the fear of overloading already top heavy class size. That was understandable. The parents of the other children feared (and unfortunately many still do) that "their bright kids" would be short-changed in the learning process by the presence of "ours." But there were some school district administrators who got it. They realized the process would take time. They spent hours in meetings with teachers and parents preparing them for the concept that all children *can* successfully go to school together. In those districts the process became a smooth transition. Now that we can see children are capable of accepting each other with their differences and schools are learning about reasonable accommodations, we are on the high road to *inclusion*.

I take comfort in the laws we have managed to pass to bring about these changes. Today's family whose child has developmental problems can stand squarely on U.S. public laws.

The Education for All Handicapped Children Act was passed in 1979. It was succeeded by IDEA, the Individuals with Disabilities Education Act. Its reauthorization has just been accomplished by Congress, after many months of honest bipartisan struggle, some compromise, and participation by patient and hardworking parent and advocate leaders. For many families the struggle may not be over, but we can score one more on the side of "better-off."

The joys of school inclusion have come too late for Barbara, but in spite of this I take heart when I see the well trained and committed teachers of her generation who have chosen special education as their field of work — some because of their early association and friendship with Barbara when they were children together many years ago. The little girl who first asked me why Barbara couldn't go to junior high with her, is now a certified counselor in one of California's Regional Centers. She loves her work and I'm proud of her. Another young woman who grew up with Barbara in our own circle of friends forty years ago is teaching students with severe disabilities in another state.

I see articles in journals based on surveys of high school students who remember their elementary school days in classes where students with disabilities were included. They experienced it as a valuable lesson in diversity that they needed to grow into thoughtful adult citizens and change agents. We the parents can count on them as future allies.

Another giant piece of federal legislation spells hope for all citizens who are affected by disabling conditions. It is the ADA or Americans with Disabilities Act. It too is a federally mandated "rock" to stand on, but it will take continuing vigilance as it "wobbles" under attacks and accusations by those who consider it too expensive to implement. The ADA not only concerns itself with physical access and accommodations such as ramps and curb cuts, lowered kitchen sinks, wider bathroom doors, and accessible public transportation, it provides access to employment for the thousands of well qualified citizens with disabilities who are now waiting to make a contribution to the world of work *as their right.*

Al and I had realized early in Barbara's life that she understood what money is for, and that work is reimbursed with it. When Al brought home papers to be collated or stapled, she would help — and also ask to be paid. But before the Americans With Disabilities Act was signed into law by President Bush in 1990, segregation still operated in the workplace. Persons with disabilities were limited to long-term sheltered work with routine, repetitive chores. This didn't do much for their self esteem and sometimes brought out behavior that was inappropriately belligerent or even self-destructive. This contributed to the public's continuing stereotypical view of our people as *incapable.*

The passage of the ADA led all of us advocates a step up the ladder of acceptance. At the ceremony of the signing, Senator Tom Harkin of Iowa said:

> With the passage of ADA, we as a society make a pledge that every child with a disability will have the opportunity to maximize his or her potential to live proud, productive and prosperous lives in the mainstream of our society.

Again the full impact of ADA was late for many of our adult sons and daughters. It did however affirm a lesson I had learned earlier from a used car dealer who had agreed to employ as a car washer a young man from the sheltered workshop. Several weeks had gone by when the vocational counselor dropped by the lot to inquire about his client. "How is Jim Walsh doing?" he asked the boss.

"Jim Walsh? I don't seem to recall—"

The counselor's heart sank. "You know, the young man I placed here from the workshop to try out for the car wash job."

"Oh yeah — Jim — I remember now. He's doing okay. He's one of us now."

Many more examples of excellence are by now scattered around Perske's "garage floor" and speak for growing acceptance of the diversity of our country's population. A community redevelopment program in Los Angeles was so successful it continued well after the federal grant which launched it ran out in 1977. It consisted of a crew of young men with developmental disabilities and a lead worker. According to one lead worker, "Some of the fellows take home blueprints and spread them out on the kitchen table to show their dads what they're doing. They may not be able to read the words, but they can point out the various components of the project and describe them. For some of the workers this has been the first time their fathers ever took an interest in anything they did." According to the project's director, "We've learned never to underestimate the personal values that come from wearing a tool belt, a hard hat and having one's own tool box. These items tell others that a guy stands ready to perform no-nonsense labor that can even be dangerous."

There were other private businesses, bravely founded by parents, that became commercially successful. A Donut Shop in southern California and a lunch counter take-out shop in Fresno set examples and spawned new concepts. Gradually many former "clients" of sheltered workshops have become "employees." They have grown in strength and courage and learned to speak for themselves. In the early days very few parents believed this could ever happen. We thought "we" would forever have to speak for "them," but this has radically changed. The young people have found their voices. *People First* has gradually evolved as a forceful organization.

I will not here attempt to write the history of the self advocacy movement. It has become another beacon of hope for parents — another answer to our perennial question of "what will happen to our sons and daughters after we are gone?" My own mentor, Gunnar Dybwad and his colleague Hank Bersani, have published *NEW VOICES, Self-Advocacy by People with Disabilities,* which records the growth of the organization — both in our country and internationally. It is expertly reported by Dybwad and Bersani, with poignant testimony by the people who have lived the life of disability.

I first learned about *People First* from the childhood friend of Barbara's who had moved to Washington State. She told me full of excitement about meetings she had attended which were organized and attended by persons with developmental disabilities. This seemed to me like a logical extension of the Youth ARC group here in California — the young volunteers and camp counselors whose enthusiasm and energy had so impressed me. I had heard them say that they did not want to be described as "serving the retarded," or "working for them." They wanted to be seen as working *with* them. So the next step had now been taken. Those with developmental disabilities were beginning to take their fate into their own hands. By the end of the seventies *People First* groups had formed in California, and I attended their first convention in San Francisco. It was a total "upper."

I had no idea Barbara would be there with her housemates and was surprised to spot her in the large hotel meeting room surrounded by a couple of hundred delegates from all over the state, and the friends from her local chapter. I had never seen such a lively, enthusiastic group of young people. They attended workshops, listened to speeches, responded with loud applause, and many walked (or rolled their wheelchairs) up to the platform to voice their own concerns and expectations. Many of the delegates had spent years of their lives in institutions and spoke of their experiences and clamored for closing institutions. Then I saw Barbara approach the platform, but she turned around at the last moment, and as she passed where I was standing I heard her say, "I chickened out." I consoled her and told her that she would have other opportunities to speak out.

I came away from this *People First* meeting convinced that the organization and many of its members were setting the pace for the future of the work that we the parents had begun. They were learning to organize meetings, take part in discussions, appear on TV and talk with legislators. They would be our allies in our "declining" years, because they knew whereof they spoke. After their passionate testimony at this convention I knew that we had moved beyond the questions, "are we better off, and do community programs work?" The question had now become, "how can we — together — make them work?"

Dear Barbara & Fred

Dear Barbara & Fred,

I wish that I could end this chapter of my life on a totally up-beat and optimistic note, but the Congress of the United States has made it difficult for me to do this. It appears bent on rolling back the supports that we have created in the last forty years and that we know have accomplished miracles of progress.

I still get up most mornings, swing my legs out of bed and find a small glimmer of hope on the horizon. It seems the State Department of Developmental Services has begun to realize respite services for families are essential underpinnings if the parents are to survive their stresses and strains intact. However, the funding is not in sync with the need.

A class action suit (Coffelt vs. Department of Developmental Services) was brought on behalf of parents who wanted their children closer to home. The case has been won, and 2,000 Development Center residents are to be moved out in five years, but the transfer process has caused bitter disagreement between the State Development Centers and the Department of Development Services and its 21 regional centers who provide these community services.

Development Center parents based their objections on a study that claimed the death rate of persons transferred into the commu-

nity far exceeds that of those who lived under the protection of the State. The community programs defend themselves.

Since the beginning of this year the San Francisco Chronicle has fanned the flames with a series of front page special reports describing abuses in community homes.

It is my hope that this current divisiveness will result in a solution to the long-standing problem of under-funding for community homes with a healthy infusion of appropriations for those who do the hands-on work. This shift in funding fairness must be accompanied by a policy of accountability by Regional Centers to the State Department and by a monitoring program with teeth that results in prompt recognition of quality where deserved and corrections where necessary. California lacks this.

Ever since my apprenticeship at Sonoma State Hospital in 1962 I have been convinced (by reading, personally observing and learning) that community programs work. People First self advocates who have lived "inside" are eloquent when they speak of their freedoms on the "outside" and wish the same for all their peers.

This transition process has succeeded in some states smaller than California, less diverse in their population and beset with fewer economic problems. New Hampshire, one example, was the first state to close "State Schools." I reviewed the videotape of the closing of Laconia State School in New Hampshire in 1991. They closed their State Schools gradually, while social policy progressed toward funding community care. There was unanimity between the components of human service providers that our people deserve to be as fully valued as do our elders, and gradually the appropriations followed. The film is called, Close the Doors, Open the Windows! People First chapters were active participants.

The Pollyanna in me hopes California's divisive situation may turn out to be the trigger to force our inflated service system to return to its initial intent; that they will trim rules, regs and reams of paper and, instead, represent all our people with developmental disabilities in their quest to live where they want to.

Yes, I have fears for the future, but that comes from being old and knowing about actuarial life expectancy figures. If I didn't face this fact squarely there is Fred to rub it in. He notices the tremor in my hands and tells me loud and clear, "You're old!" And I am old and so is Fred's father, and both of us have health problems that come with aging. It's incredibly difficult to explain to you two that even on Christmas Day our neighbor's father could have a stroke and die — and that a new baby can be born to someone, somewhere at the same time.

With luck you, Barbara, will have your sister and brother to watch over you as conservators. Guardianship or conservatorship are generally based on a court declaration of incompetence, and technically deprive the ward of many opportunities such as money contracts, changing residence without permission — even marriage. However I have no qualms at all about their judgment to watch over your life changes and decisions, and to carry out this responsibility for you in our spirit. Their emotional presence will also carry over to you, Fred.

In the meantime I choose to continue to be the burr under the saddle of bureaucrats. I write letters to legislators who don't seem to get it and I continue to attend too many endless meetings. I just can't let others' obituaries immobilize me. I try to infuse the young parents coming up with some of my knowledge and experience, and hope that it will translate into action, energy, and enthusiasm that will propel them to build on what our generation began. I hope their vision will benefit their children as well as our adult sons and daughters.

And there is good news to report on this Inauguration and Martin Luther King Day 1997. The Inauguration ceremony eased some of my recent cynicism about unpleasant national policies which threaten to affect the lives of our sons and daughters. The memory of Dr. King stirs my heart. It rekindles my idealism and gratitude to this country for welcoming me as a citizen, and enables me to continue to work and hope for the good life for citizens with disabilities.

Last weekend you two did indeed celebrate your togetherness and long-standing commitment to each other with a "Promise Party." It was a heartwarming ceremony. You were surrounded by your immediate family — Karen, David and me. Fred's dad could not come because of illness, but he was there in the spirit of love for his son. Your house family came in full force, and about a hundred other persons — a great mix of friends and staff persons from the programs you have attended, as well as a contingent of well wishers from the Mendocino Coast, the Bay Area and Sacramento. It truly felt like a community.

Barbara, you looked radiantly beautiful in white and you, Fred, proud and handsome in your new shirt and tie.

The "white" came about by your own lobbying efforts. You, Karen and I had gone shopping many weeks ago. We chose a very becoming black and white outfit with sequins that all four of us agreed on. Then you and your friends, Fred, convinced Gail that you must wear white, and another shopping trip later it was done.

The father of one of your housemates, who is a pastor, performed the ceremony in his church. He met with the two of you and talked about the meaning of faithfulness and the promise you were making to each other.

It was only the second time in my life that I witnessed a wedding where everyone applauded the processional. Karen, David and I — hand in hand — walked first. Then the two of you!

Barbara literally marched as if going on a trek, Fred followed a little behind with a high-five salute. Pastor Jon talked to you informally and with warmth. He put you at ease with his hand on your shoulders as you repeated the marriage vows after him. There was laughter when he asked for the rings. Gail who sat behind me, had them in her purse and we handed the little boxes up to the minister. When he opened them — surprise — the price tags were still attached. "Anyone got a knife?" he asked quite casually, and brother David produced one from his pocket. More applause. And more when the pastor pronounced you "partners" and you kissed.

And then the party began. It was a masterpiece of decoration and coordination. There were balloons all over the church hall, heroically *blown up by a colleague of Karen's. The food was catered, and of course it was Chinese — the absolute favorite of you all. We wished that Dr. Hall and his wife Edith (your stalwart primary physician for the first years of your life) could have been there, but he was represented by children and grandchildren. Two of the now-grown children had been camp counselors when they were teenagers, and John, one of the grandsons, volunteered to come from San Francisco to be the D.J. for the vigorous dancing. With that he continued his own commitment to the two of you, for several years ago he had invited you to his own high school prom as honored guests.*

Of course there was a beautiful three-tiered white cake (chocolate inside by request), and then another surprise! Ken Hall's white car, appropriately decorated by his wife, drove you both to a nearby motel in style. We threw birdseed at you, and I took home a generous leftover amount on which the quail in my yard are gorging themselves.

Our family and your many friends and supporters feel warm in our hearts about the event. For me it has profound meaning on two levels: it has reinforced a lesson I have learned from both the Special Olympics, and the Self-Advocacy movement over many years. A spirit of generosity, sportsmanship and true civility seems to prevail in our young people. I have seen it in sports competition and during elections for officers of People First chapters.

It happened again during the Promise Party. Gail's husband Chas, the master of ceremonies for the dance, invited those who wanted to personally congratulate you to take the mike, and they did. The "little girl" who had caused you, Barbara, such pain when she tried to compete for Fred's attention was one of them. With her hard-to-understand remarks she publicly apologized for her intrusion and wished you both well.

This has added strength to my conviction that you and other couples who live with disabilities are entitled to more than a "Promise Party." It takes me back to the young social worker whom I met many years ago at a conference in Utah, who remarked, "If we had more supported marriages we'd need fewer social workers."

It's time to take on the Federal Social Security Administration's unfair marriage penalty which flies in the face of our supposed support of family values. Our sons and daughters with disabilities face the same problems as do we who are getting older and have increasing health needs. We all need more rather than less support.

So when a couple's commitment to each other is proven over many years, and the chemistry is right as it is with you, Barbara and Fred, I can wish you no better support for your future than a loving partner in a supported marriage.

It is the same wish that I hold for Karen, David and Judy, my grandchildren Leah and Jacob, Young Al and his family and my friend Peter. Of course I'd love to know exactly what life is going to be like for you all. (I've been told that my curiosity is insatiable!) The concept of "hereafter" is particularly difficult to explain to the two of you. "I don't know" isn't good enough for something so irrevocable and natural as death, but at least I can take comfort in your firm belief, Barbara, that there is a heaven where we will all meet again.

Barbara says, "This is the People First Reunion — for people to get out of the hospital and to find a new home for them."

Lotte Moise

Lotte Moise co-founded the Paul Bunyan School for children with special needs in Fort Bragg, California. She holds a B.S. and an M.A. from Teacher's College at Columbia University and is fluent in three languages. She extended her concerns to the state, national and international levels, advocating for the poor, the elderly, and those with disabilities. She is a founding member of the North Coast Regional Center, a charter member of the Area 1 Developmental Disabilities Board, and instrumental in national organizations that assist those with developmental disabilities.

RESOURCES

Past—Present—Future

A Reading List, and More

N ow that you have read about Barbara and Fred, you may wonder where it all began, and where we are heading. For there are hundreds and thousands of persons across the land who have been part of a mighty civil rights movement these past fifty years.

Barbara uses the word "allbody," a good one that includes old parents who have been through the mill, young parents who are just getting their toes wet, those who work directly in homes and work settings with our sons and daughters, teachers, agency employees, bureaucrats, legislators, health professionals and medical researchers — many of them allies in this cause.

Because of Barbara I have witnessed much of this evolution of public awareness and consciousness raising, and the books on my shelf illustrate (in part only) the changes we have wrought. This reading and resource list is for you all. Increasingly, new technology makes information more readily available to our "People First" self advocates.

There are many other publishers who specialize in "special needs" books, i.e. Woodbine House (1-800-843-7323) and Paul H. Brookes Publishing Co., (1-800-638-3775) but the following books should get you started:

ANGEL UNAWARE, Dale Evans Rogers, 1953. The story of their little girl who lived for only two years with a severe disability. Her parents considered her a gift from heaven, to which she returned. The book shocked me. Barbara seemed so sturdy and healthy.

THE CHILD WHO NEVER GREW, Pearl S. Buck, Vineland Training School, N.J., 1950, and Woodbine House, 1992. by the Pulitzer and Noble Prize winning author, about her daughter. The new edition has an introduction by James Michener and Pearl Buck's younger daughter Janice.

CHRISTMAS IN PURGATORY; a Photographic Essay on Mental Retardation, Burton Blatt, Fred Kaplan. First published by Allyn and Bacon,1966. Then Human Policy Press, Syracuse, NY, 1974. A shocker. It depicted the conditions in a state institution, taken with a secret camera, and influenced thinking, values, principles and planning of living conditions for our people nationwide and internationally.

PERSPECTIVES ON A PARENT MOVEMENT; The Revolt of Parents of Children with Intellectual Limitations; Rosemary F. Dybwad, Brookline Books, 1990. A collection of papers and talks by one of my principal mentors.

NEW DIRECTIONS; For Parents of Persons with Mental Retardation or Other Disabilities, Robert Perske, illustrated by Martha Perske, Abingdon Press, 1973.

NEW LIFE IN THE NEIGHBORHOOD, Robert and Martha Perske, Abingdon Press, 1980.

CIRCLES OF FRIENDS; People with Disabilities and their Friends Enrich the Lives of One Another, Robert and Martha Perske, Abingdon Press, 1988.

UNEQUAL JUSTICE; What Can Happen When Persons with Retardation or Other Developmental Disabilities Encounter the Criminal Justice System, Robert Perske, Abingdon Press, 1991.

COGNITIVE COUNSELING & PERSONS WITH SPECIAL NEEDS; Adapting Behavioral Approaches to the Social Context, Herbert Lovett, Ph.D., Praeger Publishers, 1985.

LEARNING TO LISTEN; Positive Approaches and People with Difficult Be-

haviors, Herbert Lovett, Ph.D., Paul Brookes Publishing Co., 1995.

NEW VOICES; Self-Advocacy by People with Disabilities, Gunnar Dybwad & Hank Bersani, Jr., Editors, Brookline Books, 1996. We, the old parents, firmly believed that we would always have to speak for our children. This book proves us dead wrong!

COMMUNICATION UNBOUND; How Facilitated Communication Is Challenging Traditional Views of Autism and Ability/Disability, Douglas Biklen, Teachers College, Columbia University, NY, 1993. Still considered somewhat controversial by some, "F.C.," as it is referred to, opens doors of expression, thought, and poetry to persons hitherto locked in by autism and other communication disorders. I have met some of them and their parents, and attended workshops by Professor Biklen, and am a believer!

NASTY GIRLS. THUGS. AND HUMANS LIKE US; Social Relations between Severely Disabled and Non-Disabled Students in High School, Carola Murray-Seegert, Ph.D., Paul H. Brookes Publishing Co., 1989. I met the author at a convention and she confirmed that her study was based in a tough, inner-city school. If I had not already been a believer in "Inclusion," this book would have made me one!

UNDER THE EYE OF THE CLOCK; The Life Story of Christopher Nolan, Christopher Nolan, St. Martin's Press, 1987. In this book Nolan writes about himself in the third person, with a typing stick attached to his head. With amazing objectivity he describes how he freed himself of his handicap. It's an inspiration to those of us who moan and groan about our arthritis!

THE DIVING BELL AND THE BUTTERFLY, Jean Dominique Bauby, Alfred A. Knopf, 1997. Translated from the French, this little book is another one to challenge our spirit. The author was editor-in-chief of a famous French magazine when at 43 he suffered a stroke in his brain stem which left him totally non-functioning... except... Read the book and marvel.

LIFE AS WE KNOW IT, A Father, A Family, and an Exceptional Child, Michael Berube, Pantheon Books, 1996. This book amounts to a major discovery for me. Here we have a young father, forty-six years old, jumping with both feet into the parent-advocate role. Jamie is now six, has a mother and an older brother, and was hard hit with all sorts of complications when he was born with Down Syndrome. Michael Berube, a professor of English in Illinois, tells me that his close examination of policy issues surrounding his small son was more difficult than his Ph.D. in English! He talks of "representing" Jamie, a word that he has graciously permitted me to adopt. I like it better than "support" — or "advocate for." I welcome Michael Berube to the clan.

SUPPORT GROUPS AND ORGANIZATIONS

Support groups are definitely *in*. It wasn't always that way. In the late forties — before our daughter was born — a mother in Philadelphia approached a major newspaper and wanted to place an ad, asking if other parents of a daughter with mental retardation might join her for mutual support and information exchange. The paper refused to run such an ad because, they said, this would be too embarrassing and shameful!

I checked our small town weekly paper just now and found the following announcements of support group meetings: Big Brothers, Big Sisters; Humane Society; Caregiver Support Group, for those taking care of someone with memory loss and confusion; Liver support group (taking the summer off); Women's Cancer Support Group; TOPS—Taking Off Pounds Sensibly; Overeaters Anonymous; Codependents Anonymous; Building Families Through Adoption; Nicotine Anonymous.

And there is nothing anonymous about any of these groups. They are listed complete with meeting place and phone numbers!

Wherever you may live, there is bound to be a parent support group not too far away, and many of them are growing into models of coordination, direction-finding and towers of strength. This outburst of strength and energy from the younger generation of parents is useful, helpful, and hopeful because it transcends the often overly complex structure of the large organizations that we created fifty years ago. They bring moral, psychological and neighborly support back to the kitchen table where we began. Perhaps you too can start one.

Organizations abound. Their meetings, conferences and congresses in interesting locations and expensive hotels have become a major industry. Even if you could afford it, you may not have the time and energy to attend them all.

Once, years ago, Barbara, said of her house managers, "They do good things for me." That statement has become a handy yardstick to use at the end of the many endless meetings I have attended over the years: "What good things have I accomplished for Barbara today? and what are we going to do next?"

So I suggest that you look for the support organization that best fits the specific needs of your family. As I have mentioned before, we were lucky in our small rural community to have a circle of friends and neighbors. Barbara was lucky to have been born at a time and in a place on the map where good things were happening. There are many options:

THE Arc, a National Organization on Mental Retardation. P. O. Box 1047, Arlington, TX 76004. 817-261-6003; fax 817-277-3491; The Arc's Home Page on the World Web:http://TheArc.org/welcome.html   The Arc is the original parent organization in the United States and maintains branches and chapters in most States. They staff a legislative office in Washington, D.C. They publish a newsletter and are available for information to assist parents — some of it in Spanish.

NICHCY, the National Information Center for Children and Youth with Disabilities, receives thousands of inquiries each year from families, educators and others. NICHCY specializes in information about federal laws regarding education and related services, vocational training and civil rights. Call 800-695-0285 for information or a copy of a Publication Catalog. In addition many State Offices of Education publish regular newsletters.

Protection & Advocacy is a nonprofit agency that works in partnership with people with disabilities — to protect, advocate for and advance their human, legal, and service rights. It is federally funded and mandated to be an agency independent from the state in which it functions. To find out about the Protection and Advocacy Agency in your State, the services it offers, and your access to it, contact NAPAS, National Association of Protection & Advocacy Services, 900 2nd St., NE, Suite 211, Washington, DC 20002. Phone 202-408-9514, fax: 202-408-9520. (Curt Decker, Executive Director.)

TASH. The Association for Persons with Severe Handicaps, 29 W. Susquehanna Ave., Suite 210, Baltimore, MD 21204. Phone 410-828-8274, ext. 105. TASH is an international advocacy association of people with disabilities, their family members, other advocates and people who work in the disability field. TASH actively promotes the full inclusion and participation of persons with disabilities in all aspects of life. You can contact them for an information packet at the above address. They have state chapters. They are an organization with strong convictions and uncompromising goals.

UCPA — United Cerebral Palsy Associations, 1660 L Street, NW Suite 700, Washington, DC 20036-5602. Phone 1-800-USA-5UCP (1-800-872-5827), fax: 202-785-3508, email: Susannalg@aol.com   Although I am not involved with cerebral palsy as a parent, I have worked with many persons who have the condition with varying degrees of severity, and with their staff persons. I subscribe to and highly recommend the UCPA *Washington Watch — Dependable, Timely Information for America's Disability Community.* I subscribed on condition that they would stick to their four-page format! They did, and I have found it an invaluable resource.

NPND — National Parent Network on Disabilities under the guidance of Patricia McGill Smith has moved from a kitchen table in Nebraska to Washington, DC. They publish *The Friday Fax,* another concise newsletter on legislation with chapter and verse on who to write, phone or fax on issues of great importance to our sons and daughters. Their new address is 1200 G Street NW, Suite 800, Washington, DC 20005. Phone 202-434-8686, fax 202-638-0509, email npnd@cs.com

ALLIES

This is not the place for a primer on working with your legislators. We all know how important a task it is for us all, and different in every state. There are however other allies whom we should be aware of:

Judy Heuman, Assistant Secretary, U.S. Department of Education, Office of Special Education and Rehabilitative Services, is one of our strongest allies. She has lived with a disability all her life. She understands and listens. Judy Heuman 3133 Connecticut Ave., NW, Suite 427, Washington, DC 20008. Phone 202-332-5497.

Partners in Policy Making is a training academy for young parents and self-advocates. For ten years it has been training them intensively for half a year or more (with once-a-month weekend sessions) to learn the skills of advocacy and become active partners in the political and public awareness arena. It has been successful and many states support the program.

Colleen Wieck, Ph.D., Executive Director, is the person to contact for information: Minnesota Governor's Council on Developmental Disabilities, 300 Centennial Building, 658 Cedar Street, St. Paul, MN 55155. Phone 612-296-4018, fax 612-297-7200

Spectrum Institute. Sexual abuse is prevalent and of concern for our sons and daughters with disabilities. It is closely connected to the teaching of social and sexual responsibility, but I want to recommend to you a special resource person here on the West Coast. Nora J. Baladerian, Ph.D. is Director of Disability, Abuse & Personal Rights Project, Spectrum Institute, Box T, Culvert City, CA 90230-1690. Phone 310-391-2420, fax 310-390-6994, email abuses@soca.com   Dr. Baladerian works in the courts and with law enforcement. She has published material on interviewing skills to use with abuse victims who have developmental disabilities.

ADA — the Americans With Disabilities Act. Information can be accessed at the U. S. Department of Justice, Civil Rights Division, Coordination and Review Section, P.O. Box 66118, Washington, DC 20035-6118. Phone 202-514-0301 (voice), 202-514-0381 (TDD).

The problem of aging has become a major worry on the horizon of my consciousness in recent years. It's not only because I myself can feel it. (A good friend says: "Getting old is hard work— nothing but patch, patch, patch!) But because it is growing into a giant problem for the disability community.

Elvis Bozarth, P.O. Box 4011, Santa Rosa, 95402. Phone 707-578-3030, fax 707-578-0813. Elvis Bozarth is a parent, and has recently broadened his efforts from California (where he has presented to the State Developmental Disabilities Council, and works with Sonoma State University) to the National Organization on Aging, and is totally convinced (as am I) that the problem of elderly parents with dependent children is a major task ahead of us. The reality of aging will affect our sons and daughters in all aspects of their lives, from health care to residential provisions to work programs to reduced levels of independence to transportation. Elvis Bozarth is growing into an experienced advocate on this subject, but he can't do it alone. He will need many, many allies to echo his concerns and give him moral support.

ONE LAST WORD OF ADVICE

You may tell me that this book does not come close to touching your problems with disability — that I have had it easy and have learned to "work the system." You too can learn to enrich your family's life, and I have just the tool for you.

Run, do not walk, to the post office and subscribe to *Exceptional Parent, The Magazine for Families and Professionals,* — P.O. Box 3000, Dept. EP, Denville, NJ 07834-9919. For each year (12 issues, $24) you obtain a treasure trove of information and national resources that cover the full range of disabilities and conditions — cross referenced — containing email addresses and World Wide Web sites.

Each year *Exceptional Parent* publishes a Resource Guide — well over a hundred pages on technology, products and services, federal information and national advocacy resources, parent training and information centers, parent to parent programs and much, much more.

In addition you can look forward to special topics in the regular monthly issue, i.e. special education, adaptive bathrooms, directory of vans and van conversion dealers, health care, technology, summer camps and travel information, mobility and wheelchair maintenance, toys and software picks, and making friends.

It'll become your stepping stone to representing your family.